The Blessed and
Boundless God

SERIES EDITORS
Joel R. Beeke & Jay T. Collier

Interest in the Puritans continues to grow, but many people find the reading of these giants of the faith a bit unnerving. This series seeks to overcome that barrier by presenting Puritan books that are convenient in size and unintimidating in length. Each book is carefully edited with modern readers in mind, smoothing out difficult language of a bygone era while retaining the meaning of the original authors. Books for the series are thoughtfully selected to provide some of the best counsel on important subjects that people continue to wrestle with today.

The Blessed and Boundless God

George Swinnock

Edited by
J. Stephen Yuille

Reformation Heritage Books
Grand Rapids, Michigan

The Blessed and Boundless God
© 2014 by Reformation Heritage Books

Reformation Heritage Books
2965 Leonard St. NE
Grand Rapids, MI 49525
616-977-0889 / Fax 616-285-3246
orders@heritagebooks.org
www.heritagebooks.org

Printed in the United States of America
14 15 16 17 18 19/10 9 8 7 6 5 4 3 2 1

Library of Congress Cataloging-in-Publication Data

Swinnock, George, 1627-1673.
  [Treatise of the incomparableness of God in His being, attributes, works, and word, opened and applyed]
  The blessed and boundless God / George Swinnock ; edited by J. Stephen Yuille.
      pages cm. — (Puritan treasures for today)
  Originally published under title: A treatise of the incomparableness of God in His being, attributes, works, and word, opened and applyed : London : Tho. Parkhurst, 1672.
    ISBN 978-1-60178-337-0 (pbk. : alk. paper) 1. God (Christianity)—Early works to 1800. 2. God (Christianity)—Attributes—Early works to 1800. I. Yuille, J. Stephen, 1968- editor of compilation. II. Title.
  BT103.S96 2014
  231'.4—dc23
                                                    2014015067

For additional Reformed literature, request a free book list from Reformation Heritage Books at the above regular or e-mail address.

Table of Contents

Preface.. ix
Introduction.. 1

Part 1: God's Incomparable Being
1. The Excellence of God's Being.................. 9
2. Independent 11
3. Perfect....................................... 14
4. Universal 17
5. Unchangeable 19
6. Eternal 21
7. Simple....................................... 24
8. Infinite 26
9. Incomprehensible 28

Part 2: God's Incomparable Attributes
10. The Perfections of God's Nature.............. 35
11. Holiness..................................... 37
12. Wisdom..................................... 40
13. Power 44

14. Justice 47
15. Knowledge.................................. 50
16. Faithfulness................................. 55
17. Mercy 57
18. Patience 60
19. Boundless Attributes........................ 63

Part 3: God's Incomparable Works

20. The Greatness of God's Works 69
21. Creation 71
22. Providence.................................. 73
23. Redemption................................. 78
24. God Works Irresistibly 82
25. God Works Arbitrarily 84
26. God Works Effortlessly 87
27. God Works Independently.................... 90

Part 4: God's Incomparable Words

28. The Manner of God's Words.................. 95
29. The Matter of God's Words..................100
30. The Effect of God's Words...................104

Part 5: Application

31. The Malignity of Sin 111
32. The Madness of Sinners 117
33. The Misery of Sinners.......................120
34. The Folly of Pride...........................125
35. The Importance of Worship..................130
36. The Wonder of Grace 135

37. Knowing God 138
38. Sanctifying Knowledge 141
39. Satisfying Knowledge 145
40. Saving Knowledge 148
41. The Means of Attaining Knowledge 149
42. The Motives for Attaining Knowledge 153
43. Praising God 159
44. The Motives for Praising God 164
45. Incomparably Blessed 167

*For who in the heaven
can be compared unto the LORD?
Who among the sons of the mighty
can be likened unto the LORD?*
—Psalm 89:6

Preface

"Canst thou by searching find out God? canst thou find out the Almighty unto perfection? It is as high as heaven; what canst thou do? deeper than hell; what canst thou know? The measure thereof is longer than the earth, and broader than the sea" (Job 11:7–9). We have a greater chance of holding the stars in the palm of our hand, measuring the mountains on a scale, gathering the oceans in a thimble, and balancing the world's skyscrapers on a needle than we do of finding out "the Almighty unto perfection." His perfection is higher than heaven, deeper than hell, longer than the earth, and broader than the sea. Heaven is high but limited; hell is deep but restricted; the earth is long but contained; and the sea is broad but confined. God alone is unlimited, unrestricted, uncontained, and unconfined.

This boundless God "looketh on the earth, and it trembleth: he toucheth the hills, and they smoke" (Ps. 104:32). A mere glance produces earthquakes, and a mere touch produces volcanoes. If these slight impulses of God cause such devastation, what is the full effect of His power?

This boundless God "telleth the number of the stars; he calleth them all by their names" (Ps. 147:4). In the time it takes me to snap my fingers, light circles the earth seven times. Traveling at that speed, if the sun were the size of a pea, it would take ten billion years to reach the edge of the universe. How long would it take traveling at a realistic speed? How long would it take given the sun's actual size? We can't get our minds around the computation. Some astronomers estimate that there are as many stars in the universe as there are grains of sand on the earth's beaches. Here are two wonders: God can compute that number; and God can invent that number of names, one for each star.

This boundless God is a simple being. He is undivided, meaning His every thought and every action involve the whole of Him. He simultaneously gives total and undivided attention to everything and everyone. Moreover, His manifold attributes are His essence. They can no more be separated from Him than He can be separated from Himself. That means He isn't merely wise; He is wisdom. He isn't merely powerful; He is power. He isn't merely good; He is goodness. He isn't merely holy; He is holiness. He isn't merely just; He is justice. God's attributes are distinguished in their objects and effects, but they are all one in Him—His justice is His mercy, and His mercy is His justice; His wisdom is His power, and His power is His wisdom; His knowledge is His patience, and His patience is His knowledge; His wrath is His goodness, and His goodness is His wrath.

This boundless God is a sovereign being. He is the first cause of every action, impulse, thought, and breath. The motions of all His creatures depend upon His concurrence. The power that made everything maintains everything; He upholds "all things by the word of his power" (Heb. 1:3). If He were to withhold His influence, the fire wouldn't burn, the eye wouldn't see, the sun wouldn't shine, the wind wouldn't blow, the hand wouldn't move, the bird wouldn't fly, and the grass wouldn't grow. He is the principle of cohesion that holds the entire cosmos in place: "He is before all things, and by him all things consist" (Col. 1:17). It is impossible for any part of creation to exist for a moment apart from Him. He rules the universe fully and completely.

This boundless God isn't merely mighty, but almighty. He has never encountered difficulty—let alone impossibility. "None can stay his hand, or say unto him, what doest thou?" (Dan. 4:35). He knows what was, what is, what will be, what can be, and what can't be. By one pure, simple, eternal act of His infinite understanding, He knows all things perfectly, immediately, and distinctly—at every moment.

There is no proportion between this boundless God and our bound intellect, between this limitless God and our limited mind, between this infinite God and our finite understanding. Those who hear Him most clearly hear but a faint whisper. Those who see Him most fully see but a small glimmer. Those who understand most about Him understand nothing in comparison to what there is to be known. God does "marvellous things without number" (Job 5:9). Can we "find out" God? We're like small children standing on the beach, trying in vain to hold the ocean in a bucket.

Do we have any effect upon this boundless God? Does He need us? Does He gain anything from us? "Can a man be profitable unto God?" (Job 22:2). He is a perfect being, meaning He is incapable of increase or decrease. Nothing can be added to Him or subtracted from Him. He doesn't require anything outside of Himself, nor does He benefit from anything outside of Himself. Our effect upon God is that of a snowball hurled at the blazing sun. What are we to God?

"Hell and destruction are before the LORD: how much more then the hearts of the children of men?" (Prov. 15:11). God peers into the heart—weighing its desires, motives, impulses, and inclinations. He sees a heart riddled with self-love. This sin is an affront to Him—a transgression of His law, a rejection of His rule, a desecration of His goodness, and a violation of His glory. He has power to avenge Himself. He can cast us into hell with a mere look. A day is coming when He will deal definitively with sin. He "shall bring every work into judgment, with every secret thing, whether it be good, or whether it be evil" (Eccl. 12:14). He is a perfect judge with unsearchable knowledge of the evidence and unrivaled power to execute the sentence.

Amazingly, this boundless God draws near to us in the incarnation. The Son of God clothed Himself with our humanity. He whom the heavens cannot contain was contained in the womb of a woman. He came so close that He experienced life in a fallen world. The Bread of Life was hungry, and the Water of Life was thirsty. He came so close that He bore our sin and shame and tasted death for us (Heb. 2:9). We placed ourselves where this boundless God deserves to be—on the throne. This boundless God placed Himself where we deserve to be—on the cross. His forgiveness supersedes our sinfulness, His merit eclipses our guilt, and His righteousness hides our vileness. His abundant mercy blots out our multitude of transgressions (Ps. 51:1).

By virtue of our union with Christ, we draw near to this boundless God. We find in Him all we could ever want. We find an eternal and spiritual good, suitable to our every need. We rest in Him as the dearest Father, wisest Guide, strongest Shield, greatest Good, closest Friend, richest Grace, highest Honor, kindest Comfort, finest Beauty, deepest Truth, and sweetest Love. Our knowledge of this boundless God diffuses into our soul a satisfying peace in this life and a ravishing foretaste of what awaits us in glory.

In brief, that is the message of George Swinnock's *The Blessed and Boundless God.*[1] His text is Psalm 89:6: "For who in the heaven can be compared unto the LORD? who among the sons of the mighty can be likened unto the LORD?" From the psalmist's assertion that no one in heaven or earth is like God, Swinnock derives his principal doctrine—namely, God is incomparable. In chapters 1–30, he proves his doctrine by demonstrating God's incomparableness in His being, attributes, works, and words. In chapters 31–45, he applies his doctrine by demonstrating how God's incomparableness informs, counsels, and comforts us.

This is a tremendous book. Without question, Swinnock is a consummate theologian—steeped in Scripture, proficient in the arts and philosophies, and familiar with a wide spectrum of theological writers. But equally important is the fact that Swinnock is a pastor-theologian. That is to say, the aim of his theological inquiry is always the people of God. He views theology neither as a mere intellectual or theoretical exercise nor

---

1. George Swinnock was born in 1627 at Maidstone, Kent. He was a graduate of Cambridge (BA) and Oxford (MA). He was a pastor until his death in 1672. His writings are available in *The Works of George Swinnock*, ed. James Nichol, 5 vols. (1868; repr., Edinburgh: Banner of Truth, 1992). Nichol's edition contains all of Swinnock's writings except *The Life and Death of Mr. Thomas Wilson, Minister of Maidstone, in the County of Kent, M.A.* (London, 1672). The original title for the present work is *The Incomparableness of God*. It is found in volume 4 of Swinnock's *Works*.

as a mere academic pursuit, but he sees it as the means by which we grow in acquaintance with God and, consequently, in godliness. For Swinnock, therefore, the goal of theology is to engage the mind with the ultimate purpose of embracing the heart's innermost affections.

I unreservedly recommend this book to you and encourage you to read it prayerfully, thoughtfully, and expectantly, keeping in mind Swinnock's simple conviction that "when we take the incomparable God as our God, we are incomparably blessed."

J. Stephen Yuille

Introduction

Our eternal happiness consists in large part in our perfect knowledge of the blessed and boundless God. When we "see him as he is," we will be like Him in holiness and happiness (1 John 3:2). We will be fully satisfied with His love and likeness. Our noblest faculty (our understanding) will derive matchless delight from its intimate acquaintance with the greatest truth: God.

Our present holiness also depends a great deal upon our knowledge of God. According to the apostle Paul, all people are "alienated from the life of God through the ignorance that is in them, because of the blindness of their heart" (Eph. 4:18). In other words, people wander from God because they do not know Him. Dark corners of a house are filled with dust, dark cellars with vermin, and dark hearts with lusts. But when we come to know God, we desire Him. We know His beauty and bounty and love Him. We know His power and faithfulness and trust Him (Ps. 9:10). Moreover, we trample on the treasures of this world and endure the loss of our possessions "joyfully" (Heb. 10:34) because we know God, who is "true riches" and "unsearchable riches" (Luke 16:11; Eph. 3:8). Like Moses, we refuse to be called the sons of kings' daughters (condemning honors and spurning crowns) because we know God is our crown of glory (Heb. 11:24–25). We look to the Lord of glory, who so infinitely excels all earthly glory. Comparably speaking, we "hate" father, mother, spouse, children, and life itself, entrusting everything to our Maker because He is better than the whole creation (Luke 14:26). When "the God of glory" appeared to him, Abraham quickly and quietly left his country and family without hesitation (Acts 7:2–4). Similarly, all earthly glories fade when God makes Himself known to us. These stars vanish when the Sun of Righteousness appears.

Our Lord Jesus declares, "And this is life eternal, that they might know thee the only true God, and Jesus Christ, whom thou hast sent" (John 17:3). Knowing God is the principle of spiritual life and the start of eternal life. But who can know God when He infinitely surpasses all knowledge? It is true that the magnitude of God's perfections is well beyond the reach of our finite understanding, but we can know what He has chosen to reveal. The starting point for such knowledge is the psalmist's declaration: "For who in the heaven can be compared unto the LORD? who among the sons of the mighty can be likened unto the LORD?" (Ps. 89:6).

The causal particle "for" connects this verse to the previous verse: "And the heavens shall praise thy wonders, O LORD: thy faithfulness also in the congregation of the saints." The "heavens" (that is, the angels) rejoice in the church's welfare and praise God for preserving His people and fulfilling His promises. In our verse, the psalmist elaborates on the cause of this praise by pointing to God's incomparable excellence.

"Who in the heaven can be compared unto the LORD?" Some people interpret "heaven" as referring to the sun, moon, and stars. They believe the psalmist's point is that none of these luminaries can compare to "the Father of lights" (James 1:17). While that assertion is true, it is far more likely the psalmist is speaking of the heaven of heavens (the third heaven)—the dwelling place of the celestial spirits: cherubim and seraphim, angels and archangels, principalities and powers, thrones and dominions. Who among the innumerable company of angels can compare to the Father of spirits? Considered simply in themselves, angels are glorious creatures in respect to their power, wisdom, purity, and beauty, but considered comparatively with the blessed God, their glory is nothing.

"Who among the sons of the mighty can be likened unto the LORD?" The "sons of the mighty" are the greatest rulers on earth. Elsewhere, they are described as "gods" and "children of the Most High" (Ps. 82:6). Yet they are nothing in comparison to God.

In these two questions, the psalmist challenges heaven and earth to bring forth anyone equal to God. Who in heaven or earth can be "compared" or "likened" to "the LORD"? The name "LORD" is *Jehovah*—God's proper name. It signifies that He was and is and is to come. He is always the same, and He is the cause of all other beings (Ps. 102:26–28; Acts 17:28; Rev. 1:4–6).

The doctrine that emerges from the psalmist's questions is this: God is incomparable. There is no one among the highest and holiest in heaven or earth like Him. The most excellent beings fall infinitely short of this Being of beings.

"Among the gods there is none like unto thee, O Lord" (Ps. 86:8). Here, the psalmist does not compare God with the lowest but the highest. These "gods" include demons. They are the gods of this world, and they are the princes of the powers of the air (2 Cor. 4:4; Eph. 2:2). They are like the Antichrist, "who opposeth and exalteth himself above all that is called God, or that is worshipped; so that he as God sitteth in the temple of God, showing himself that he is God" (2 Thess. 2:4). But among these demons, "there is none like unto thee, O Lord." They are not even worthy to be mentioned in the same breath with the high and holy God.

These "gods" also include idols. Idols of gold and silver have mouths but cannot speak; they have eyes but cannot see; they have ears but cannot hear; they have noses but cannot smell; they have hands but cannot handle; and they have feet but cannot walk (Ps. 115:4–7). Idols are the work of humans, who are themselves infinitely below their Creator. Therefore, "we know that an idol is nothing in the world, and that there is none other God but one" (1 Cor. 8:4).

These "gods" also include angels and rulers (Pss. 8:5; 82:6). God has stamped His image upon them in that they exercise authority and dominion over others. But among them, "there is none like to thee, O Lord." They are "gods" by derivation and deputation, meaning their authority comes from God. They remain weak creatures, limited by God's precepts and liable to God's judgments. Their essence is from God, their subsistence is by Him, and their dependence is upon Him. God alone is the Most High: "higher than the highest" (Eccl. 5:8).

God is incomparable. The truth of this doctrine is clearly evident when we consider His being, attributes, works, and words.

PART 1

God's Incomparable Being

CHAPTER 1

The Excellence of God's Being

To begin with, God is incomparable in His being. He has an excellency in His being; therefore, He is called "his excellency" (Job 13:11). God's "name alone is excellent" (Ps. 148:13). His "name" refers to anything by which He makes Himself known. In this instance, "name" specifically refers to God's being (that is, God Himself). "The name of the LORD is a strong tower" (Prov. 18:10)—that is, God Himself is a strong tower. "His name is great in Israel" (Ps. 76:1)—that is, God Himself is great in Israel. Only His being is excellent, because there is no other being like His. He is excellent in all, above all, and beyond all.

God's name declares the incomparable nature of His being. "And God said unto Moses, I AM THAT I AM: and he said, Thus shalt thou say unto the children of Israel, I AM hath sent me unto you" (Ex. 3:14). God is I AM—a being that really is, and there is no other besides Him. What human or angel can say I AM? None, for this is the proper name of God.

When God promises Himself as a reward to His people, He does so under the notion of being, essence, or substance, in opposition to all other beings which are but shadows in comparison to Him. "I lead in the way of righteousness, in the midst of the paths of judgment: that I may cause those that love me to inherit substance" (Prov. 8:20–21). God will cause those who love Him to possess what is. God is, and all other beings are nothing in comparison to Him. "Behold, the nations are as a drop of a bucket, and are counted as the small dust of the balance: behold, he taketh up the isles as a very little thing.... All nations before him are as nothing; and they are counted to him less than nothing, and vanity" (Isa. 40:15, 17). If we were able to conceive of the idea of anything being less than nothing, then we would understand what all things are in comparison to God.

CHAPTER 2

Independent

God is an independent being. He is from Himself, meaning He is His own first cause. Angels and humans are derivative beings. The apostle Paul tells us that we are indebted to God for our beings: "For in him we live, and move, and have our being" (Acts 17:28). We were nothing until God spoke us into being (Gen. 2:7; Job 10:11–12; Ps. 139:13–15). The whole world is His work-manship (Acts 17:24). The greatest angel is as indebted to God for his being as the smallest atom: "For by him were all things created, that are in heaven, and that are in earth, visible and invisible, whether they be thrones, or dominions, or principalities, or powers" (Col. 1:16). But God is indebted to no one for His being. He was when no one else was—even from eternity (Ps. 90:1). "I am the LORD, and there is none else" (Isa. 45:6). He is what He is of Himself and from Himself.

As God is His own first cause, so He is His own last end. As He is wholly from Himself, so He is wholly for Himself. All other beings are for another: "All things were created by him, and for him" (Col. 1:16). Since all things are from God, it only stands to reason that they must also be for God. Good people and angels are for God and exist for His glory (Isa. 6:3; Rom. 14:7–8). Evil people and angels are also for God—not in their intentions, but in His intention by His wise and powerful government over them: "The LORD hath made all things for himself: yea, even the wicked for the day of evil" (Prov. 16:4). All beings are "of him, and through him, and to him" (Rom. 11:36). But God is altogether for Himself as His highest end. He is His own end as well as His own beginning. He never had a "beginning" nor will He ever have an "ending" (Rev. 1:8). He does what He does for Himself: "Thou art worthy, O Lord, to receive glory and honour and power: for thou hast created all things, and for thy pleasure they are and were created" (Rev. 4:11). Similarly, He is what He is for Himself. He is a wise, infinite, almighty, everlasting, unchangeable, holy, righteous, and faithful being for Himself. It is the excellency and purity of saints and angels to be what they are and to do what they do for God—to make Him the final cause of their beings and actions. But it is the excellency and purity of God to be what He is and to do what He does *for Himself*. He who is His own happiness must be His own end.

Finally, God is by Himself. No one in heaven or earth contributes anything to God, the Lord of the whole world. "If I were hungry, I would not tell thee: for the world is mine, and the fulness thereof" (Ps. 50:12). Here, He declares to the world that He is incapable of the least need. He challenges the world to produce anyone who ever helped Him: "Who hath prevented me, that I should repay him? whatsoever is under the whole heaven is mine" (Job 41:11). Where is the creature who can claim he ever did the least kindness to God?

All other beings are dependent. The highest and strongest are not able to bear their own weight, but—like ivy—they must have something upon which to lean: "By him all things consist" (Col. 1:17). As the beams depend on the sun and the streams depend on the fountain, so creatures depend on God for all things. He upholds "all things by the word of his power" (Heb. 1:3). He is the Atlas who bears up the whole world—without Him it would fall into nothing. God is to the world as the soul is to the body. He animates and actuates everything in it, and He enables His creatures in all their motions. We are apt to think that fire can burn by itself because it is so natural for it to burn. Yet if God were to suspend His influence, a furnace heated seven times hotter than usual would burn no more than water (Dan. 3:27). We are apt to think that a man can see by himself as long as his eye is rightly disposed. Yet if God were to deny His concurrence, a man would see no more than if he were stark blind (Gen. 19:11; 2 Kings 6:18). "O LORD, thou preservest man and beast" (Ps. 36:6).

CHAPTER 3

Perfect

God is a perfect being. When we describe a being as perfect, we mean one of two things. First, a being is perfect when it possesses all that is necessary to its kind (that is, its particular species). So we say a man is perfect because he has all that is necessary to a man—a body with all its parts and members, and a soul with all its powers and faculties. Second, a being is perfect when it is impossible to add to it or take from it. That is to say, it is incapable of the least increase or decrease.

God alone is perfect in the second sense. He is absolutely perfect. The sun neither gains anything when the moon is bright nor loses anything when the moon is dark. Likewise, the self-sufficient God neither gains anything from our service nor loses anything by our neglect. He is above the influence of our actions. Our holiness adds nothing to His happiness: "Can a man be profitable unto God, as he that is wise may be profitable unto himself? Is it any pleasure to the Almighty, that thou art righteous? or is it gain to him, that thou makest thy ways perfect?" (Job 22:2–3). As our holiness does not help Him, so our sinfulness does not hurt Him: "If thou sinnest, what doest thou against him? or if thy transgressions be multiplied, what doest thou unto him? If thou be righteous, what givest thou him? or what receiveth he of thine hand? Thy wickedness may hurt a man as thou art; and thy righteousness may profit the son of man" (Job 35:6–8). The weapons of unrighteousness might injure flesh and blood, but not the Rock of Ages. He is impenetrable.

God is also above our praises and blessings. What does a fountain gain if people drink its water and commend it rather than despise it? What would God gain if He were to make millions of worlds to magnify Him? What would God lose if there were no world at all? "Who hath first given to him, and it shall be recompensed unto him again?" (Rom. 11:35). God has given to everyone all that they possess, but no one has ever given anything to Him. When we give Him our love, awe, and trust, we actually give Him nothing. We can give nothing to Him because we owe everything to Him. All of our giving, praising, and serving add nothing to Him. His essential glory admits no increase or decrease.

No other being is absolutely perfect like God. We stand in continual need. We need air to sustain us, food to strengthen us, clothing to cover us, fire to warm us, and sleep to refresh us. We need righteousness to justify us, grace to sanctify us, love to comfort us, and mercy to save us. We are a heap of infirmities, a hospital of diseases, and a bundle of imperfections.

Angels are more perfect than we are, yet they too are imperfect. Something can be added to them, and something can be taken from them. The highest angel can be higher, the holiest angel holier, and the best angel better. Although the stars differ from each other in brightness, none of them are the sun. Although angels differ from each other in honor and excellency, none of them are God—none of them are absolutely perfect.

CHAPTER 4

Universal

God is a universal being. All good is in Him virtually and eminently. The many excellencies scattered among the creatures of heaven and earth are united in an infinite manner in the Creator. This is a truth of philosophy: whatever good is in the effect is more abundantly in the cause. Since God is the cause of all the good in His creatures, then all this good must exist even more abundantly in Him.

That is why Scripture compares God to whatever is good. At times, Scripture compares Him to that good which is essential: life, light, food, water, and rest (Pss. 36:9; 116:7; John 1:4, 9; 4:10; 6:51; James 1:17). At times, Scripture compares Him to that good which is beneficial: home, health, peace, fire, and refuge (Pss. 42:11; 57:1; 90:1; Zech. 2:5; 2 Cor. 13:11). At other times, Scripture compares Him to that good which is delightful: wealth, honor, joy, and pleasure (Job 22:24– 25; Ps. 43:4; Isa. 33:21; Zech. 2:5). He is compared to wine, which is the delight of the palate (Isa. 25:6);

beauty, which is the delight of the eyes (Song 5:10–16); fragrance, which is the delight of the nostrils (Song 4:10); music, which is the delight of the ears (Song 5:6, 16); truth, which is the delight of the understanding (Ps. 31:5; John 14:6); and good, which is the delight of the will (Matt. 19:17).

God is not one single good, but all good. The truth is that our excellencies are not even a shadow to set off God's excellencies. We are limited beings: "How much less man, that is a worm? and the son of man, which is a worm?" (Job 25:6). There is some good in one person and some good in another person, but there is not all good in any person. All good is in God (Mark 10:18).

CHAPTER 5

Unchangeable

God is an unchangeable being. He is incapable of the least alteration. He is the same yesterday, today, and forever (Heb. 13:8). He is eternally what He was and what He will be. He is today as He was before the universe was made and as He will be after the universe is remade. With Him there "is no variableness, neither shadow of turning" (James 1:17). Here, James speaks of the sun, moon, and stars. The term "variableness" refers to these bodies' declensions and revolutions, which result in shadows. James's point is that these lights are variable, but the "Father of lights" is not. He experiences no rising or setting, no increasing or decreasing. He always shines with the same light and luster—the same beauty and brightness.

When God made the angels pure and holy, He loved them. Subsequently, He hated those angels who rebelled. But God did not change. When we set clay under the sun, it hardens. When we set wax under the sun, it softens. In neither case does the sun change.

When God punishes a wicked man and then blesses him upon his repentance, He remains the same. If a person walks on one side of a church, the pillars are on his left; if he walks on the other side, the pillars are on his right. But the pillars remain where they are. The motion or change is in the person.

The heavens seem constant, but their perpetual motion reveals their perpetual alteration: "They shall perish, but thou shalt endure: yea, all of them shall wax old like a garment; as a vesture shalt thou change them, and they shall be changed: but thou art the same, and thy years shall have no end" (Ps. 102:26–27). The old heavens will pass away and new ones will replace them, but the God of heaven will never pass away. Angels are changeable. They can lose what they have and attain what they have not. They are mutable in regards to place—sometimes in heaven and sometimes on earth. We too are changeable. We are in constant motion from one condition to another. The body changes—at last into dust and corruption (Job 17:14). The soul changes in its affections: love, hate, delight, and desire. We do not continue to be what we were (Job 14:2–3). The world is always ebbing and flowing, but the Maker of the world declares, "I am the LORD, I change not" (Mal. 3:6).

CHAPTER 6

Eternal

Time has a beginning and an ending—it belongs to all creatures in this world. Aeviternity has a beginning but no ending—it belongs to angels and humans.[1] Eternity has no beginning, succession, or ending—it belongs to God alone.

For starters, God has no beginning. He created the heavens and earth "in the beginning" (Gen. 1:1). "Before the mountains were brought forth, or ever thou hadst formed the earth and the world, even from everlasting to everlasting, thou art God" (Ps. 90:2). It puzzles the mind to conceive of God's duration: "Behold, God is great, and we know him not, neither can the number of his years be searched out" (Job 36:26).

Furthermore, God has no succession. He dwells in one indivisible point of eternity. He is what He is in one

---

1. *Aeviternity* is a philosophical term used to describe the condition of angels and humans. Their existence lies between the eternal (God) and the temporal (material things).

infinite moment of being. His duration knows nothing of former or latter, past or future. His essence is not bound, but He enjoys His whole eternity every moment. He inhabits eternity (Isa. 57:15). "Beloved, be not ignorant of this one thing, that one day is with the Lord as a thousand years, and a thousand years as one day" (2 Peter 3:8). He inhabits a million years in one moment, and each moment to Him is as a million years.

Nothing has been added to God's duration since the creation of the world. It is incorrect to say "God was," for none of His duration is ever past with Him. It is also incorrect to say "God will be," for none of His duration is ever future with Him. His name is I AM (Ex. 3:14), not I WAS or I WILL BE. His full eternity is always present. Christ declares to the Jews: "Before Abraham was, I am" (John 8:58). It seems like poor grammar, but it is proper theology. If an angel had spoken, it would have been proper for him to say: "Before Abraham was, I was." If Adam had been alive in Christ's day, it would have been proper for him to say: "Before Abraham was, I was." But it was most proper for Christ (who is God) to say, "Before Abraham was, I am." His duration is without any succession—the whole of it is ever present.

"Thou art my Son: this day have I begotten thee" (Ps. 2:7). These words refer to the eternal generation of the Son of God. They also refer to His resurrection (Acts 13:33). Both are present "this day" with God. That which had no beginning (His Son's eternal generation) was not past to Him, and that which was to come (His Son's temporal resurrection) was not future to Him. Both are always before Him: "This day have I begotten thee."

Finally, God has no ending. He is "from everlasting to everlasting" (Ps. 90:2). His years "shall have no end" (Ps. 102:27). That is to say, He alone possesses immortality (1 Tim. 6:16).

Are angels comparable to God? No, they had a beginning (Col. 1:16), and they have a succession in their duration. They enjoy part today, part tomorrow, and part the next day. They do not enjoy what is past or what is to come, but only what is present. Are we comparable to God? No, we are here today and gone tomorrow (Job 14:1). Our days are like grass (Ps. 103:15). We quickly flourish and perish. There is a vast difference in duration between God and us. "Are thy days as the days of man? Are thy years as man's days?" (Job 10:5). Our days begin, succeed, and end, but God's days do not. Even if David had lived as long as Methuselah, he could still say, "Mine age is as nothing before thee" (Ps. 39:5).

CHAPTER 7

Simple

God is a simple being. I do not use the term *simple* to suggest that God is not wise, for in Him "are hid all the treasures of wisdom and knowledge" (Col. 2:3). I use it in reference to mixture and composition. The simpler something is, the more excellent it is. God is a most simple, unmixed, and indivisible essence. He is incapable of the least composition and, therefore, of the least division. He is most pure—without parts, members, or qualities. Whatever is in Him is His very being. We can attribute any quality of a human or angel to God in the abstract. Humans and angels are wise, but God is wisdom (Prov. 9:1). Humans and angels are holy, but God is holiness (Isa. 63:15). God is all being and nothing else.

How unlike God are humans and angels! We are compounded beings. We are compounded of body and soul (Gen. 2:7). Our body is compounded of parts and members. Our parts and members are compounded of blood, flesh, skin, bones, and sinews (Job 10:11). Our soul is compounded of substance and accidents—essence and faculties. The substance and qualities of the soul are distinct things. Our wisdom is one thing; our power is another; our holiness is another. And these are all distinct from our essence. Our understanding differs from our will, our will differs from our affections, and our affections differ from both. And all these differ from our being. But all these are one indivisible essence in God. They are all one and the same in Him.

CHAPTER 8

Infinite

God is an infinite being. He is without bounds or limits, measures or degrees. God is a sphere whose center is everywhere and whose circumference is nowhere. "But will God indeed dwell on the earth? behold, the heaven and heaven of heavens cannot contain thee; how much less this house that I have builded" (1 Kings 8:27). The "heaven of heavens" cannot contain the God of heaven. No place can define Him. He is not shut in or shut out of any place. He is without place, yet in all places.

> Whither shall I go from thy spirit? Or whither shall I flee from thy presence? If I ascend up into heaven, thou art there: if I make my bed in hell, behold, thou art there. If I take the wings of the morning, and dwell in the uttermost parts of the sea; even there shall thy hand lead me, and thy right hand shall hold me. (Ps. 139:7–10)

God is in heaven, hell, earth, sea, and infinitely more, meaning He is where there is no heaven, no hell, no earth, and no sea.

God is boundless in His duration, perfections, attributes, and being. No place can circumscribe Him. He is "above all" by His dominion, "through all" by His providence, and "in…all" by His essence (Eph. 4:6). He is everywhere—not virtually as the sun by its beams, not authoritatively as a king by his officers, not by motion as animate creatures move from one place to another, not by mixture as the air mingles with the terrestrial world, but essentially after an unspeakable manner. God is whole in the whole world, and He is whole in every part of the world. If He were to make ten thousand worlds, His whole essence would be in every part of each world, yet without the least motion, extension, or multiplication.

Are humans and angels like God? No, they are finite beings. We fill a small place to the exclusion of all others, and we are limited to it. Angels are in a finite compass beyond which their beings do not extend. They are in one place and not another. If they are in heaven, they are not on earth at the same time. But God is everywhere in His whole essence at every moment: He "filleth all in all" (Eph. 1:23).

CHAPTER 9

Incomprehensible

God is an incomprehensible being. No creature—human or angelic—can understand Him perfectly. If God is infinite, then He must necessarily be incomprehensible, for the finite can never comprehend the infinite. There is no proportion between a bounded understanding and a boundless being. The sun may sooner be contained in a small crack and the ocean in a small shell than God in our limited understanding.

> Hell is naked before him…. [He] hangeth the earth upon nothing. He bindeth up the waters in his thick clouds; and the cloud is not rent under them…. He hath compassed the waters with bounds…. The pillars of heaven tremble and are astonished at his reproof…. Lo, these are parts of his ways: but how little a portion is heard of him? (Job 26:6–14)

What we know of God in comparison to what is to be known is but a drop to the vast ocean and a whisper to the loud thunder. "How little a portion is heard of him?"

Surely, we hear a great deal of Him from the voice of
creation and providence, and especially from the voice
of His Word. Unbelievers hear a little (Rom. 1:20–21),
saints on earth hear much more (Ps. 63:3–6), and saints
in heaven hear most of all (1 Cor. 13:12; 2 Cor. 12:3–4).
But how little is heard of Him in comparison to the
excellency that is in Him?

The being of God is like the peace of God "which
passeth all understanding" (Phil. 4:7). It is like the love of
Christ "which passeth knowledge" (Eph. 3:19). The only
thing that can be known of God is that He can never
be fully known. "Canst thou by searching find out God?
canst thou find out the Almighty unto perfection? It is
as high as heaven; what canst thou do? deeper than hell;
what canst thou know? The measure thereof is longer
than the earth, and broader than the sea" (Job 11:7–9).

"Canst thou by searching find out God?" It is
impossible to find out God. Zophar's point is that a
mere human cannot contain and comprehend God,
whom the heaven of heavens cannot contain or comprehend. Are we so foolish as to think that the short
line of our understanding can fathom God's bottomless
being? It is not in vain for us to seek Him, but it is altogether in vain for us to search Him. Although He is not
far from us, He is far above and beyond us—far above
our thoughts and conceptions. God dwells "in the light
which no man can approach unto; whom no man hath
seen, nor can see" (1 Tim. 6:16). In this sense, darkness

surrounds Him. On a dark day, we see the beams but not the body of the sun; likewise, in heaven, the angels see God's beams but not His infinite being.

"Canst thou find out the Almighty unto perfection?" If we seek for God, we will find Him (Prov. 8:17; Matt. 7:7), but we will not find Him unto perfection. The word "perfection" signifies utmost accomplishment. We can know something of God, but we cannot know all of Him. Whoever finds out the most is still far from finding out the utmost. We will sooner grasp the sun and stars in our hands and measure the hills and mountains in the scales before we will "find out the Almighty unto perfection." If natural questions challenge the greatest scholars, how much more must divine questions exceed human understanding! "As thou knowest not what is the way of the spirit, nor how the bones do grow in the womb of her that is with child: even so thou knowest not the works of God who maketh all" (Eccl. 11:5).

"It is as high as heaven; what canst thou do?" We cannot reach heaven's heights with our short arms. The most high God is far higher than the highest heavens. He is above and beyond all. Who knows the nature, number, order, and motion of the heavenly bodies? Who knows anything of the worship of the celestial courtiers in the third heaven? Who knows the One who orders, preserves, governs, animates, and actuates all things? Who knows the One who upholds all things and enables them to do all that they do? Who knows God?

"Deeper than hell; what canst thou know?" Heaven and hell are the greatest distance apart, and they are most remote from our understanding. Who knows what is done in heaven or hell? Who knows what is enjoyed in the one and suffered in the other? Does anyone know the misery of the damned—the extremity, universality, and eternality of their torment? Who has returned from that place to tell us what they suffer? Even if someone had, whose understanding is large enough to perceive it? "Who knoweth the power of thine anger? even according to thy fear, so is thy wrath" (Ps. 90:11). Does anyone know God who "setteth an end to darkness, and searcheth out all perfection: the stones of darkness, and the shadow of death" (Job 28:3)? Does anyone know the God before whom hell and destruction are open and naked? Does anyone know the God who lays the dark vault of hell and stores it with fire, brimstone, darkness, and all the instruments of eternal death?

"The measure thereof is longer than the earth, and broader than the sea." The earth is long from one end to the other, but the knowledge of God is much longer. The ocean is exceedingly wide. David calls it a "great and wide sea, wherein are things creeping innumerable, both small and great beasts" (Ps. 104:25). But the knowledge of the great God is far wider. The heavens are high, yet their height is finite. Hell is deep, yet its depth is determined. The earth is long, yet its length is limited. The sea is broad, yet its breadth has bounds. But God is beyond all these. His measure is beyond all measure.

PART 2

God's Incomparable Attributes

CHAPTER 10

The Perfections of God's Nature

God's attributes are those perfections in the divine nature which are ascribed to Him so that we can better understand Him. They are called *attributes* because they are attributed to Him for our sake, even though they are not in Him as they are in humans or angels.

Some of God's attributes are incommunicable because they cannot be attributed to humans or angels. I spoke of these under God's being in chapters 1–9. It is impossible for a mere creature to be infinite, independent, or incomprehensible. God is incomparable in these excellencies. Pride and presumption led Satan and Adam to rival God in His incommunicable properties—to aspire to be like Him in His sovereignty. Their sin was that they desired to be their own lords and masters. God charges the prince of Tyre with unforgiveable arrogance: "Thou has set thine heart as the heart of God" (Ezek. 28:6).

Some of God's attributes are communicable because He communicates them to humans and angels. It is the nature of godliness to be like God in these attributes. David is called a man after God's own heart because he was a man after God's own holiness. The new man is created "after God"—the re-impression of His image upon us (Eph. 4:24). Conformity to God in His communicable attributes is our perfection and happiness in heaven (Ps. 17:15). But even in these, we fall infinitely short of Him.

CHAPTER 11

Holiness

God is incomparable in His holiness. In general, the term *holiness* refers to an object's moral goodness or its agreement with its rule. Holiness in the creature is its conformity to the will of its Creator in the principle, rule, and end of its actions and motions. Holiness in God is that excellence of the divine nature by which He acts from Himself, for Himself, and according to His own will. God is "the Holy One" (Hosea 11:9) by way of eminence and excellence because He surpasses all others in holiness. He is "holy, holy, holy" (Isa. 6:3; Rev. 4:8).

God's nature is the only pattern of holiness; therefore, He commands us to look to Him as our example: "Be ye holy; for I am holy" (1 Peter 1:16). God made us holy—according to His image (Gen. 1:26; Eccl. 7:29; Eph. 4:24). His will is the only rule of holiness. For this reason, Scripture describes our holiness as proving "what is that good, and acceptable, and perfect, will of God" (Rom. 12:2) and as walking according to His Word (Gal. 6:16).

God is universally holy in His name, nature, works, and law (Ps. 145:17; Hab. 1:13; Luke 1:49; Rom. 7:12). He is the original of all holiness in humans and angels. He is the only reason they are not as unholy as the demons. But what human or angel is comparable to God in holiness? "Who is like unto thee, O LORD, among the gods? who is like thee, glorious in holiness?" (Ex. 15:11). "Behold, he putteth no trust in his saints [the holiest on earth]; yea, the heavens [the holiest in heaven] are not clean in his sight" (Job 15:15). We are a sink of sin—covered from head to foot with the leprosy of sin (Gen. 6:5). Instead of comparing ourselves with God, we ought to abhor ourselves for our lack of holiness. As for the angels, they have nothing amiss in their natures. They have remained God's loyal subjects and faithful servants, and they have observed all His calls and commands. As a matter of fact, Scripture sets forth their obedience as an example to us (Matt. 6:10). Yet they are unholy in comparison to God: "The heavens are not clean in his sight" (Job 15:15). By "heavens," Job's friend Eliphaz does not mean only the place, which possesses a relative holiness because of God's special presence, but also the angels. They have no blemish in their beings or disorder in their motions, yet they are unclean in God's sight. The holiness of angels is found in obeying a law, but the holiness of God is being the law (Ps. 103:20–21; 1 Thess. 4:3). The holiness of angels is found in conforming to a pattern, but the holiness of God is being the pattern. The holiness of angels is derivative, but the holiness of God is original.

God is so incomparable in holiness that He alone is holy: "Who shall not fear thee, O Lord, and glorify thy name? For thou only art holy" (Rev. 15:4). No one is holy besides Him because no one is holy like Him. "There is none holy as the LORD: for there is none beside thee" (1 Sam. 2:2). Saints are holy (1 Peter 2:9) and angels are holy (Mark 8:38), but they are not holy as God is holy. Without question, the heavenly hosts, who see Him face to face and are satisfied with His likeness, are glorious in holiness. They shine brightly with those perfect beams which they borrow from the Sun of Righteousness. But they are mere glowworms in comparison to "the Father of lights" (James 1:17). The holiness of saints and angels—which infinitely surpasses the heavens in beauty and brightness—is nothing in comparison to the holiness of God.

CHAPTER 12

Wisdom

God is incomparable in His wisdom. In general, wisdom entails perceiving things accurately and then taking action in accordance with those correct perceptions. Wisdom appears chiefly in three acts: The first is *knowledge*—discerning the nature, causes, and effects of things. The second is *understanding*—identifying the highest and noblest ends in our actions. The third is *prudence*—ordering the best means for attaining those ends. Like the rudder of the ship, prudence steers and directs the course of life. In each of these respects, God is incomparable in wisdom. "He is wise in heart" (Job 9:4), meaning He is most wise because the heart is the seat of wisdom.

In God "are hid all the treasures of wisdom and knowledge" (Col. 2:3). A treasure denotes something that is precious: gold (not dust) is a treasure. It also denotes something that is plentiful: a bag (not a piece) of gold is a treasure. God's wisdom is precious; therefore, it is described as counsel—the effect of serious and mature deliberation (Isa. 9:6; Eph. 1:11). God's wisdom is also plentiful. In Him are all the "treasures" of wisdom. A treasure denotes abundance, but "treasures" speak of superabundance. His wisdom is "manifold" (Eph. 3:10); it is embroidered wisdom in which there is rich variety. "With him is wisdom and strength, he hath counsel and understanding" (Job 12:13).

Some people are wise. Daniel possessed "light and understanding and excellent wisdom" (Dan. 5:14). David understood "more than the ancients" (Ps. 119:100). Solomon exceeded all others in wisdom: "God gave Solomon wisdom and understanding exceeding much, and largeness of heart, even as the sand that is on the sea shore. And Solomon's wisdom excelled the wisdom of all the children of the east country, and all the wisdom of Egypt. For he was wiser than all men" (1 Kings 4:29–31). But was Solomon comparable to God in wisdom? He "was wiser than all men," yet he was a stark fool in comparison to God. "For the wisdom of this world is foolishness with God" (1 Cor. 3:19). Our wisdom is sheer folly before God: "The foolishness of God is wiser than men" (1 Cor. 1:25). If it were possible for any folly to be in God or for any of God's actions to be foolish, He would still be wiser than the brightest among us.

Angels are wise. The excellency of their natures bespeaks the excellency of their wisdom. But are they anything like God? No, they are fools in comparison to Him: "Behold, he put no trust in his servants;

and his angels he charged with folly" (Job 4:18). They never manifested the least folly in any action, but they are accused of folly in comparison to God. They are not guilty of actual folly but potential folly. That is to say, they are not guilty of absolute folly but comparative folly.

God so far exceeds angels and humans in wisdom that He is called "only wise" (Rom. 16:27; 1 Tim. 1:17). Wisdom belongs to Him alone. The wisest humans and angels need a master to teach them and a tutor to instruct them. If not for the only wise God, they would be as foolish as the wild donkey's colt. But God is above all teachers and tutors: "Shall any teach God knowledge?" (Job 21:22). Some people are incapable of receiving instruction because of their extreme weakness—their ability is so low that they cannot learn. But God is incapable of receiving instruction because of His immense wisdom—His ability is so high that there is nothing for Him to learn.

"Who hath directed the Spirit of the LORD, or being his counsellor hath taught him?" (Isa. 40:13). The wisest rulers receive counsel from advisors. The reason is obvious: "Two are better than one" (Eccl. 4:9). But God is all understanding. He does not need anyone to advise Him. Two candles are better than one, but one sun is better than a million candles because its light is incapable of the least addition. "With whom took he counsel, and who instructed him, and taught him in the path of judgment, and taught him knowledge, and shewed to him the way of understanding?" (Isa. 40:14). Who has counseled God? Who has taught Him what is just and unjust? Who has taught Him how to govern the affairs of this world and in what manner and measure to order everyone's portion? Who has directed God? Who has taught God a single lesson? "For who hath known the mind of the Lord? or who hath been his counsellor? or who hath first given to him, and it shall be recompensed unto him again?" (Rom. 11:34–35).

CHAPTER 13

Power

God is incomparable in His power. Power is that force or ability by which we act. God's power is that attribute by which He effects whatever He pleases. "O LORD God of hosts, who is a strong LORD like unto thee?" (Ps. 89:8). He is not only strong but also "mighty in strength" (Job 9:4); He is not only powerful but also "excellent in power" (Job 37:23). "If I speak of strength, lo, he is strong" (Job 9:19). God never contends without prevailing, and He never fights without conquering. He is strong indeed.

When God acts, there is no standing before Him: "He doeth according to his will in the army of heaven, and among the inhabitants of the earth: and none can stay his hand" (Dan. 4:35). God can stop the strongest creature in its fullest motion, but no one can stop Him in His actions. Many people seek to oppose Him, but none of them have power to overcome Him. When God acts, there is no striving with Him: "When thou passest through the waters, I will be with thee; and through the rivers, they shall not overflow thee" (Isa. 43:2). The floods of the ungodly might be violent, but they can never overcome those whom God protects. He is their shield of defense (Gen. 15:1).

David declares, "God hath spoken once; twice have I heard this; that power belongeth unto God" (Ps. 62:11). Certainly, it is an extraordinary thing that David introduces his statement with such a preface: "God hath spoken once; twice have I heard this." What had he heard? "Power belongeth unto God." Power is God's peculiar excellence. He is not only mighty, but almighty; not only the mighty God, but the almighty God (Isa. 9:6; 2 Cor. 6:18). He has never met with difficulty, much less with impossibility. All things are hard for us, and many things are hard for angels, but nothing is too hard for God. "I know that thou canst do every thing" (Job 42:2).

Some people are strong, but is their strength anything like God's power? No, for "the weakness of God is stronger than men" (1 Cor. 1:25). The apostle Paul is not suggesting there is any weakness in God. He is speaking of those actions in which God is pleased to conceal His power. Even this "weakness" far excels human strength. God challenges Job: "Hast thou an arm like God?" (Job 40:9). The arm is that instrument by which we exert and exercise our power. Job has a strong arm—he is "the greatest of all the men of the east" (Job 1:3; 29:25). But does he have an arm like God? Can he give life and take life and lift up and cast down at his pleasure? Is his arm long enough to reach his enemies and strong enough to break them in pieces with a single blow? Can he wield a sword with his arm to the terror, horror, confusion, and destruction of all his opponents? Does Job have an arm like God? No, as the psalmist says, "Thou hast a mighty arm: strong is thy hand, and high is thy right hand" (Ps. 89:13).

Angels are stronger than humans. Evil angels are principalities and powers, fierce lions, and great dragons (Eph. 6:12; 1 Peter 5:8; Rev. 12:9). These descriptions indicate that their power is far superior to ours. The devil is "the prince of the power of the air" (Eph. 2:2). He can command storms and tempests and blow down houses and cities. Yet evil angels are fettered in the chains of God's anger and power. They cannot break free. In all likelihood, good angels are even stronger than evil angels. One of them destroyed 185,000 men in a single night (2 Kings 19:35). They "excel in strength" (Ps. 103:20). The spirituality and purity of their nature bespeaks their power. Yet despite their power, they are weak in comparison to God. They acknowledge His power above all others (Rev. 4:11). God's power has no equal, no parallel. There is no "rock like our God" (1 Sam. 2:2).

CHAPTER 14

Justice

God is incomparable in His justice. In general, justice means giving people what they deserve. God's justice is that attribute whereby He disposes all things according to the rule of equity and renders to all people according to their works (Deut. 32:4; Job 34:11; Ps. 62:12; Gal. 6:7). He is eminently just: the "Just One" (Acts 7:52). He is superlatively just: the "most just" (Job 34:17). He is altogether just without any shadow of injustice. He is just in the highest degree—beyond all degrees.

God gives all people their due without "respect of persons" (2 Chron. 19:7). He does not stand in awe of anyone for their power or greatness. He "accepteth not the persons of princes, nor regardeth the rich more than the poor" (Job 34:19). God judges according to a just law (Rom. 2:12–16; 7:12); therefore, He is most just. "Yea, surely God will not do wickedly, neither will the Almighty pervert judgment" (Job 34:12). People might do justly, but God must do justly because His will is His law. He is the most exact rule of all justice and righteousness. Whatever He does is just, because He is the great supreme and sovereign of the world (Job 34:13).

God's actions are occasionally mysterious, but they are always righteous. "The LORD is righteous in all his ways, and holy in all his works" (Ps. 145:17). When His "way is in the sea," His "path [is] in the great waters," and His "footsteps are not known" (Ps. 77:19), even then "all his ways are judgment" (Deut. 32:4)—not judgment as opposed to mercy, but judgment as opposed to injustice. When clouds and darkness surround Him (that is, when His providences are such hard texts that no one can expound them, and such dark riddles that no one can unfold them) even then "justice and judgment are the habitation of [His] throne" (Ps. 89:14). His disposing power always moves within the sphere of righteousness.

People can be just; for example, Noah, Joseph, John, and Cornelius were just (Gen. 6:9; Matt. 1:19; Mark 6:20; Acts 10:22). But "shall mortal man be more just than God? shall a man be more pure than his maker?" (Job 4:17). It is presumptuous for us to prefer ourselves before God (Isa. 14:13–14), and it is monstrous impudence for us to compare ourselves with God; to compare a weak creature to the almighty Creator is to compare crookedness to straightness or darkness to light. The most just among us are unjust in comparison to God. "For in thy sight shall no man living be justified" (Ps. 143:2). We might be just in the sight of others, but we are unjust in the sight of God. When we compare a candle with the sun, it is nothing—it must hide its head in shame. Likewise, what is a godly person when compared with God? "But how should man be just with God? If he will contend with him, he cannot answer him one of a thousand" (Job 9:2–3). That is to say, we cannot even present one just act out of a thousand. How then can we be just before God?

Angels are just—they are righteous in their natures. But are they righteous before God? Although they are just in comparison to us, they are unjust in comparison to God (Job 4:18). Angels are capable of actual injustice, but God is not. The law (or rule) of their righteousness is outside them; therefore, they are capable of swerving from it. But the law (or rule) of God's righteousness is inside Him. He is His own law, so it is impossible for Him to err from it.

God's will is the rule by which He acts. Therefore, His every action is just. He can never err in anything He does, because His will is the rule of all He does. Such is the creature's weakness that he might wander out of his way, but such is the Creator's power and perfection that He cannot possibly wander. He is His own way. "He doeth according to his will in the army of heaven, and among the inhabitants of the earth" (Dan. 4:35). He acts according to His essential eternal rule. God so surpasses humans and angels in justice that He is said to be the habitation of justice: "They have sinned against the LORD, the habitation of justice" (Jer. 50:7). Justice dwells nowhere but in Him and with Him.

CHAPTER 15

Knowledge

God is incomparable in His knowledge. Knowledge is that attribute of God whereby He understands all things in and of Himself. Scripture attributes eyes and ears to God, because He is an eyewitness of all that is done and an "ear-witness" of all that is said (2 Chron. 16:9; Ps. 11:7). God's understanding is like His being: boundless. "His understanding is infinite" (Ps. 147:5). "For the LORD is a God of knowledge, and by him actions are weighed" (1 Sam. 2:3). The expression "God of knowledge" points to the greatness of His knowledge. He is "perfect in knowledge" (Job 37:16). This is not only true comparatively (as one person may be perfect in respect to another), but it is also true absolutely. His knowledge is so perfect that it cannot increase or decrease.

Some people are knowledgeable. Solomon was famous for his knowledge (2 Chron. 1:12). For example, he could speak of the nature of all plants—from the cedar to the hyssop (1 Kings 4:33). Angels are even more knowledgeable. They have sharper wits and quicker apprehensions. Elect angels surely know much more than evil angels, for they always behold the face of God. They behold in that face (as in a glass) more than we can discern or evil angels can conceive. Since their understandings are of a larger capacity and their natures are more excellent, angels know even more than the saints who are in heaven.

But does anyone know as God knows? Can it be said of any human or angel that he is "perfect in knowledge"—that his knowledge is incapable of increase or decrease? Can it be said of any human or angel that his knowledge is infinite? Our knowledge in this world is little in comparison to what it will be: "For we are but of yesterday, and know nothing" (Job 8:9). We are not here for long, and we have but little experience; therefore, we have but little knowledge—so little that it is called "nothing." The knowledge of saints and angels in heaven is enough for their perfection and satisfaction, but it is still so little in comparison to the knowledge of God. Finite knowledge is nothing when compared with infinite knowledge.

As for the matter of God's knowledge, He is incomparable. He knows all things (John 21:17). "God is greater than our heart, and knoweth all things" (1 John 3:20). He knows what was, what is, what will be, what can be, and what cannot be. He knows all substances, qualities, and contingents. He creates, upholds, governs, and discerns everything. "For the eyes of the

LORD run to and fro throughout the whole earth"
(2 Chron. 16:9).

God knows those things that are secret and hidden—
the feelings, thoughts, and motions of the soul. "For
what man knoweth the things of a man, save the spirit
of a man which is in him?" (1 Cor. 2:11). What angel
knows "the things of a man?" Not one. But God knows.
"Hell and destruction are before the LORD: how much
more then the hearts of the children of men?" (Prov.
15:11). Hell seems to be far from God's sight. Similarly, the human heart seems to be unsearchable—so
deep that no one can fathom it. But God sees into
these depths. He knows our hearts better than we
know ourselves. "The heart is deceitful above all things,
and desperately wicked: who can know it? I the LORD
search the heart" (Jer. 17:9–10). No one knows it but
God. "For thou, even thou only, knowest the hearts of
all the children of men" (1 Kings 8:39). It is His sole
prerogative. Humans and angels may see faces, bodies,
garments, etc.—all those things seen from the outside.
But God sees the inside. He pries into the very heart
(1 Sam. 16:7). All things are "naked and opened" before
Him (Heb. 4:13; cf. 1 Chron. 28:9; Jer. 11:20).

God knows the past, present, and future. "Thou
knowest my downsitting and mine uprising, thou under-
standest my thought afar off" (Ps. 139:2). Long before
we think our thoughts, they are in God's thoughts. We
do not know what a day will "bring forth" (Prov. 27:1),

but God knows what is in the womb of eternity. He knows what all ages and generations will produce. He declares "the end from the beginning, and from ancient times the things that are not yet done" (Isa. 46:10). Predictions are secret things which belong to God alone (Isa. 41:22–26).

As for the manner of God's knowledge, He is incomparable. He knows all things completely and perfectly. Humans and angels know what they know incompletely and imperfectly. They only know a part of what is knowable, and even this they only know in part. But God beholds everything thoroughly (2 Chron. 16:9). He has a distinct, certain, and thorough knowledge of all things.

God knows all things by immediate intuition. We know things by sense (eyes, ears, etc.), faith, discourse, or instruction. God knows one thing by another: the conclusion by its premises, the cause by its effects, and the consequence by its antecedents. He knows all things in themselves, and He sees all things in Himself. We require a twofold light in order to see: a light in the eye and a light in the air. But "the Father of lights" (James 1:17) needs no light in order to see: "The darkness and the light are both alike to thee" (Ps. 139:12).

God knows all things at once. We know one thing by another and one thing after another. Our understandings are unable to take in very many objects at once, much less all objects at once. But God sees all things at one view: "The LORD looketh from heaven; he beholdeth all the sons of men. From the place of his habitation he looketh upon all the inhabitants of the earth" (Ps. 33:13–14). We can see multiple things at once, but we must move our eyes in order to see more things. Similarly, our minds must move from thought to thought in order to focus on a single object. But God takes in everything distinctly and particularly at once.

God knows all things from everlasting—before the world existed. Humans and angels can know what is and when it is, but they cannot know it before it was. "Known unto God are all his works from the beginning of the world" (Acts 15:18). Before He constructed the frame of this world, He knew all the motions and actions of its inhabitants. By one pure, simple, undivided, and eternal act of His understanding, He knows all things perfectly, immediately, and distinctly at every moment.

CHAPTER 16

Faithfulness

God is incomparable in His faithfulness. Truth is that attribute of God whereby He is in Himself as He reveals Himself to be, and He is in His speaking and acting as He speaks and acts. He is truly eternal, immutable, and infinite. He is the true God in opposition to false gods (Jer. 10:10; John 17:3; 1 Thess. 1:9). He is truth because He is the unchangeable archetype of all true things outside Himself. He is truth because His eternal decrees are certain (Ps. 33:11). He is never deceived or disappointed in His purposes.

God is truth toward His creatures. In His works, all He does is true; His actions of creation, providence, and redemption are real (Deut. 32:4; Pss. 25:10; 111:7; Rev. 15:3). In His words, all He says is true; His precepts, promises, and predictions are true (Josh. 23:14; Ps. 119:86, 142; Isa. 55:3; Hab. 2:3). God is truth itself (John 14:6). He is "abundant" in truth (Ex. 34:6), and He is the "God of truth" (Ps. 31:5). He is a God "that cannot lie" (Titus 1:2). At times, lying arises from forgetfulness; some people break their word because their memories are poor. But God never forgets. At times, lying arises from weakness; some people want to keep their promises, but they lack the ability to do so because their circumstances have changed. But God never changes. At times, lying arises from wickedness; some people are able to keep their word, but they refuse to do so. But God never breaks a promise. He cannot be accused of wickedness: "There is no unrighteousness in him" (Ps. 92:15).

People can be true. But what are we in comparison to God? "Men of high degree are a lie: to be laid in the balance, they are altogether lighter than vanity" (Ps. 62:9). Angels are true. But if we consider them as they are in themselves, we see it is possible for them to lie. However, it is "impossible for God to lie" (Heb. 6:18). God is so true that He only is true (Rom. 3:4).

CHAPTER 17

Mercy

God is incomparable in His mercy. God knows Himself, loves Himself, and glorifies Himself, but He is not merciful to Himself. God's mercy, therefore, is an attribute that relates to us. God's justice seeks a worthy object, God's grace seeks an unworthy object, but God's mercy seeks a needy object. God is gracious to elect angels, because they cannot merit their perfection and happiness. But He is not merciful to them, for they were never in a state of misery. Fallen man is the proper object of God's mercy. We are undeserving of the least good, having plunged ourselves into all evil. Mercy is an attribute of God whereby He pities us in our misery. He has "tender mercies" (Ps. 25:6). He is "afflicted" in His people's afflictions (Isa. 63:9). As parents are extremely troubled on account of their children's afflictions, so God "pitieth them that fear him" (Ps. 103:13). But not only does He pity us in our misery, He relieves us. God's mercy has a hand to supply as well as a heart to pity.

God glories in His mercy (Ex. 33:19). Judgment is "his strange work" (Isa. 28:21). He does not "afflict willingly" (Lam. 3:33). In other words, it is not His nature to disturb and destroy people. It is their sin that forces thunderbolts into His hands. He "delighteth in mercy" (Mic. 7:18). The blessed God has a "multitude" of mercies (Ps. 51:1) to answer the multitude of our sins. He has "abundant mercy" (1 Peter 1:3). He is "rich in mercy" (Eph. 2:4). "His tender mercies are over all his works" (Ps. 145:9). His mercy inspires all admiration: "How excellent is thy loving-kindness" (Ps. 36:7). And His mercy defies all apprehension: "For thy mercy is great above the heavens" (Ps. 108:4). He is "the Father of mercies" (2 Cor. 1:3).

Mercy is God's joy and pleasure, His glory and honor. When Moses desires to see His glory, God proclaims, "The LORD God, merciful and gracious" (Ex. 34:6–7). When God promises to do merciful things for His people, He says it will be to Him "a name of joy" (Jer. 33:9). He is universally merciful: "All the paths of the LORD are mercy and truth" (Ps. 25:10). He is merciful at all times and in all respects (Ps. 118:1; Eph. 1:3; 1 Tim. 6:13; 2 Peter 1:3–4). He is "rich in mercy" (Eph. 2:4).

People are merciful, and so are angels in a sense. But none of them can compare to God. The tender mercies of the righteous—even of angels—are cruelties in comparison to God's mercies. Do we have the depth of pity that God has? Do we have the power and ability to relieve the afflicted like God does? Do we possess preserving and protecting mercy (Job 10:12), pardoning and forgiving mercy (Mic. 7:18), purifying and renewing mercy (Eph. 2:4), saving and sanctifying mercy (Titus 3:5–6)? How infinitely short do we come of God! He is so incomparable in mercy that mercy belongs to Him alone: "Unto thee, O Lord, belongeth mercy" (Ps. 62:12).

CHAPTER 18

Patience

God is incomparable in His patience. Patience is that attribute of God whereby He bears with sinners, deferring their punishment or awaiting their conversion. He is "slow to anger" (Ps. 103:8). He is long-suffering (2 Peter 3:9). He endures vessels of wrath with "much long-suffering" (Rom. 9:22). He waits, "that he may be gracious unto you" (Isa. 30:18). God's patience is even more admirable when we consider the following.

First, God hates sin (Ps. 5:4; Prov. 6:16–19; Hab. 1:13). It grieves Him (Eph. 4:30). He is so infinitely perfect that no sin can hurt Him, but He is so infinitely pure that all sin is offensive to Him. Sin is contempt for His authority, equivalent to despising Him (1 Sam. 2:30), dishonoring Him (Rom. 2:23), and fighting against Him (Job 15:25). It is a violation of God's commands, so it is *transgression* (1 John 3:4). Sin is an affront to His wisdom, so it is *foolishness* (2 Sam. 24:10); it is an affront to His justice, so it is *unrighteousness* (1 John 1:9); and it is an affront to His truth, so it is *deceit* (Isa. 44:20).

Sin is an affront to His patience, so it is described as despising His long-suffering (Rom. 2:4). It is an affront to His mercy, so it is described as turning His grace into debauchery (Jude 4).

Second, God sees sinners. He knows our sins—their nature and number. He knows our thoughts, desires, words, and actions. "For I know your manifold transgressions and your mighty sins" (Amos 5:12). We are His creatures. He loves us inconceivably (John 3:16) and blesses us bountifully (Ps. 116:12). He seeks to overcome us daily with His kindness (Ps. 130:4), but we are rebels and traitors. We join with Satan in seeking God's ruin (Eph. 2:2–3). God has the power to avenge Himself whenever He pleases. He can look, speak, and think us into hell. But here is a wonder: God is "great in power" yet "slow to anger" (Nah. 1:3).

Third, sinners provoke God's patience. Good men quarrel with His providence (Ps. 73:2–4; Jer. 12:1–3), and evil men continue in their sin while accusing Him of indifference (Eccl. 8:11). Despite these provocations, God forbears and continues to do good to His creatures. He provides life, health, food, shelter, friends, and families. He sends the gospel, seasons of grace, and offers of His love (Acts 17:26–28; 2 Cor. 5:19–20).

Some people are patient. For example, Moses was the meekest man on the earth (Num. 12:3). Yet even Moses grew impatient when the Israelites "provoked his spirit" (Ps. 106:33). If God were as impatient as we are, there would be no hope for us. But God is so incomparable in His patience that He is called "the God of patience" (Rom. 15:5). He has all manner of patience in Him.

CHAPTER 19

Boundless Attributes

Although God grants holiness, wisdom, power, justice, and other qualities to us in some measure, He remains incomparable in His communicable attributes. Why?

First, these attributes are essential to God. They are from Him and in Him. In other words, He is their author and subject. He is not indebted to anyone for them. He can thank only Himself that He has them. But these attributes are derivative in us. Justice, wisdom, and holiness are in us, but they are not from us. They come from God. When God humbles Job, He does so by manifesting the vast difference between them. He says, "Deck thyself now with majesty and excellency; and array thyself with glory and beauty" (Job 40:10). The terms "deck" and "array" mean to clothe. They convey the idea of abundance; for example, to be "clothed with shame" is to be extremely ashamed (Ps. 35:26), and to be "clothed with humility" is to be extremely humble (1 Peter 5:5). The terms "deck" and "array" also convey the idea of visibility. We cannot go outside without people seeing our clothes. And so Job has acted as if there were no great distance between him and God. He has acted as if he were equal to God. God challenges him to prove it: "Deck thyself now with majesty and excellency; and array thyself with glory and beauty." God can clothe Himself with these things in the highest degree. He is "clothed with honour and majesty" (Ps. 104:1). He has covered Himself "with light as with a garment" (Ps. 104:2). If Job can do what God has done, then he has the right to compare himself with God.

Second, these attributes are the very essence of God. They are not qualities or properties as they are in humans and angels. The holiness of God is the holy God. "Once have I sworn by my holiness" (Ps. 89:35). When God swears by His holiness, He swears by Himself. The power of God is the powerful God. The truth of God is the true God. The wisdom of God is the wise God. All His attributes are His essence. In humans and angels, wisdom, power, and justice are properties. These properties differ from their substances. This is apparent in the fact that many humans and angels exist without these attributes. Their essence and properties can be separated. An angel can be an angel without being holy, wise, or just. A human can be a human without being powerful, patient, or merciful. The reason is because these properties are distinct from the essences of humans and angels. But in God, His attributes are His very essence. They are Him; therefore, they can no more be separated from Him than He can be separated from Himself. God could not be God if He were not most wise, most holy, most just, and so on. God's attributes make up one pure essence which is made manifest to us in many ways. God's punishment of the wicked is His justice. God's performance of His promises is His faithfulness. God's salvation of the miserable is His mercy. God's forbearance of the guilty is His patience. All of these are His essence—Himself.

Third, these attributes are all one in God. For example, His justice is His mercy, His wisdom is His patience, and His knowledge is His faithfulness. These attributes are distinguished in regard to their objects and effects, but they are all one in Him. They are His essence, and His essence is a pure undivided being. In humans and angels, these attributes are distinguishable from one another, for we can have one without the other. Our righteousness is one thing, our power a second thing, and our patience a third thing. Some people have one of these attributes while lacking the others. But in God, they are all one and the same. When sunbeams shine through a yellow glass, they are yellow; when through a green glass, they are green; when through a red glass, they are red; yet all the while the sunbeams are the same. When the sun shines on clay, it hardens it; on wax, it softens it; on flowers, it draws out fragrant smells; on ditches, it draws out repugnant odors; yet it is the same sun. The difference lies in the objects and effects. Likewise, God is always working in the world. When He punishes the obstinate, He is righteous. When He saves the penitent, He is merciful. Yet He is the same immutable God.

Fourth, these attributes are in the highest degree in God. They are limited in us, because a finite substance cannot admit of an infinite property. But immensity runs through God's properties. His understanding is infinite, along with His justice, mercy, power, and all other attributes. They have no limits but His pleasure. He has never put forth so much power that He could not put forth more if He so pleased. He has never exercised so much patience that He could not exercise more if He so pleased. This is why God's attributes are affirmed in the abstract: He is not only loving; He is love (1 John 4:8). He is not only wise; He is wisdom (Prov. 9:1). He is not only good; He is goodness (Ex. 33:19). He is not only holy; He is holiness (Isa. 63:15). Because these attributes are God's being, they are boundless.

PART 3

God's Incomparable Works

CHAPTER 20

The Greatness of
God's Works

"O Lord GOD, thou hast begun to show to thy servant thy greatness, and thy mighty hand: for what God is there in heaven or in earth, that can do according to thy works, and according to thy might?" (Deut. 3:24). God is incomparable in His works. He does "wonders" (Ex. 15:11) and "wondrous things" (Ps. 86:10). He is "excellent in working" (Isa. 28:29). His work is "great" (Joel 2:21), "perfect" (Deut. 32:4), "honorable and glorious" (Ps. 111:3). "God thundereth marvellously with his voice; great things doeth he, which we cannot comprehend" (Job 37:5).

The works of humans and angels are small things which we perform through divine concurrence. But God's works are great and unsearchable. We cannot comprehend them. "O the depth of the riches both of the wisdom and knowledge of God! how unsearchable are his judgments, and his ways past finding out!" (Rom. 11:33). His "footsteps are not known" (Ps. 77:19). He "doeth great things and unsearchable; marvellous things without number" (Job 5:9). We can easily count the great works we do. Together, they are nothing in comparison to the least of God's great works. His ways are not our ways: "For as the heavens are higher than the earth, so are my ways higher than your ways, and my thoughts than your thoughts" (Isa. 55:9). None of our ways are like His ways, and none of our works are like His works (Ps. 86:8). This is true of both the matter and manner of His working.

CHAPTER 21

Creation

God is incomparable in His work of creation. The creature cannot create. We can alter the form, but we cannot produce the matter. A goldsmith can make a sparkling jewel, but he requires precious stones to do so. He cannot make gold out of dust, or diamonds out of dirt. We cannot create one grain of corn or one blade of grass. We can put the matter into a better form, but we cannot make matter when there is none.

But God can. He produced all things out of nothing. He erected the stately fabric of heaven and earth and all the creatures that dwell in them. In so doing, He proves that He is the true God, "the living God, which made heaven, and earth, and the sea, and all things that are therein" (Acts 14:15). "He hath made the earth by his power, he hath established the world by his wisdom, and hath stretched out the heavens by his discretion" (Jer. 10:12). Can anyone be so foolish as to imagine that anything can compare with God, the Creator of all things?

When God proclaims His sovereignty and excellency to Job, He challenges him: "Where wast thou when I laid the foundations of the earth? declare, if thou hast understanding. Who hath laid the measures thereof, if thou knowest? or who hath stretched the line upon it?" (Job 38:4–5). God points to the precision of His works by speaking of lines and measures. His principal intent is to show His omnipotence and our impotence: "Where wast thou when I laid the foundations of the earth?" Did anyone lend God a helping hand?

God made the innumerable creatures in the earth, ocean, and sky out of nothing. "Through faith we understand that the worlds were framed by the word of God, so that things which are seen were not made of things which do appear" (Heb. 11:3). The great God had no materials with which to make the great house. He did not frame it from any preexistent matter (Isa. 45:12). Yet all creation evidences such admirable matter and form, subjects and properties, power and goodness, wisdom and order. It possesses rare beauty, harmony, and symmetry. It is difficult to determine which part of creation caused the psalmist to cry: "O LORD, how manifold are thy works! in wisdom hast thou made them all: the earth is full of thy riches" (Ps. 104:24).

CHAPTER 22

Providence

God is incomparable in His work of providence. To begin with, He is the "preserver of men" (Job 7:20). When masons and carpenters build houses, they leave much of the work in others' hands. But God maintains what He constructs. His providence is indeed a continual creation: "By him all things consist" (Col. 1:17). The hand that made everything maintains everything. The power that produced all things out of nothing must preserve all things from returning to nothing. The being that gave us our beings must uphold us in our beings: "In him we live, and move, and have our being" (Acts 17:28).

God upholds "all things by the word of his power" (Heb. 1:3). How? First, He upholds all things as the foundation upon which they stand. He "hangeth the earth upon nothing" (Job 26:7). This means His power is the only pillar that supports it. Second, He upholds all things as the fountain from which they derive their motion. The motions of all His creatures depend upon His concurrence. If He were to suspend His influence, the fire would not burn, the eye would not see, and the sun would not shine (Job 9:7). Third, He upholds all things as the bond by which they hold together. Like a vessel to water, He keeps all things from flowing away to their dissolution. It would be impossible for the creation (or any part of it) to exist even for a moment if God were to deny His concurrence to it. God is to the world as the soul is to the body. He alone moves and actuates it. Without Him, the world cannot stir. It is but a dead corpse.

In addition to preserving, God governs creation. No creature governs itself. If God did not maintain unity and harmony by guiding all things in their motions and directing all things to their ends, the world would soon fall into chaos. "The LORD hath prepared his throne in the heavens; and his kingdom ruleth over all" (Ps. 103:19). Apart from God's governance, one creature would prey on another—the whole earth would turn into a field of blood. If God did not guide and govern, the order of nature would give way to confusion and destruction.

God governs the highest creatures, even monarchs and governors. Some rulers think their hands are their own to do as they please. But they cannot command their hands because God rules their hands. Herod and Pilate were gathered together to do whatever God's hand and counsel "determined before to be done" (Acts 4:27–28). Some rulers think their hearts are their own to will as they please. But they cannot command their hearts because God rules their hearts. "The king's heart is in the hand of the LORD, as the rivers of water: he turneth it whithersoever he will" (Prov. 21:1). God turns the king's heart whichever way He chooses, the way that most magnifies His glory. "A man's heart deviseth his way: but the LORD directeth his steps" (Prov. 16:9). No man is his own master—he is not even master of his own thoughts.

God also governs the lowest creatures. As none are so high as to be above His precepts, so none are so low as to be below His providence. "Are not two sparrows sold for a farthing? and one of them shall not fall on the ground without your Father" (Matt. 10:29). Sparrows appear to fly freely and fall casually, but God actually directs their flight and orders their fall. They neither fly nor fall accidentally; it all occurs providentially.

God also governs the most stubborn creatures. The winds seem to scorn all authority, but they are at God's command (Ps. 148:8). When they rush forth with such irresistible force that nothing can stand before them, God rides on their wings. He turns them at His pleasure (Pss. 18:10; 104:3). He causes them to blow (Ps. 147:18). He holds them in His fist (Prov. 30:4). He can hold them fast or let them loose. The waves seem even more uncontrollable than the winds. But God "sitteth upon the flood" (Ps. 29:10), forcing obedience and submission. He "hath bound the waters in a garment"

(Prov. 30:4). He binds the water like a woman wraps her baby in a blanket. The ocean swallows thousands, burying them in its belly. When it roars and rages, everyone trembles. But God orders it as He pleases. He can put it to sleep in an instant—no matter how wild it is. It does not stir without His permission. God "set bars and doors, and said, Hitherto shalt thou come, but no further: and here shall thy proud waves be stayed" (Job 38:10–11).

Some people are extremely stubborn—as immoveable as rocks. Their wills are fixed and their ways are resolved. But God commands them at His pleasure. The king of Babylon was an untamable beast. He had foraged many countries and kingdoms and trampled on many false gods. He came against the people of God like a lion greedily attacking its prey. He came to tear them into pieces. But God had this monster at His command: "Therefore will I put my hook into thy nose, and my bridle in thy lips, and I will turn thee back by the way by which thou camest" (Isa. 37:29). Because the king raves like a huge unruly fish, God catches him with His hook. Because he rages like a fierce wild animal, God bridles him with His bit. God curbs, leads, and draws the king of Babylon wherever He pleases.

The demons are even more uncontrollable than people. They have great power (Luke 11:21). They act in union, thereby increasing their strength. Although there are thousands of them, they unite against God as if they were one. They have observed people for thousands of years. As a result, they are very cunning. Because they hate God, they employ all their power to oppose Him. They seek to break out from under His yoke. Yet in spite of all their might and malice, God governs them as a jailor oversees his prisoners in chains. "He hath reserved [them] in everlasting chains under darkness unto the judgment of the great day" (Jude 6). What does this mean? First, it means they are bound by their own terrifying consciences, which give them no rest day or night. All times are dark and dreadful for them, and all places are dark and dismal. Second, it means they are bound by chains of divine providence. God governs their persons and motions. They only go where He pleases. They cannot even touch swine without His permission (Matt. 8:31).

CHAPTER 23

Redemption

God is incomparable in His work of redemption. His works of creation and providence are subordinate to this masterpiece. His attributes sparkle most gloriously in it (Ps. 102:16); His angels in heaven admire and adore Him for it (Rev. 4:10–11). It is the work of all His works, from which He reaps so much glory (Isa. 43:21). Together, angels and humans could not redeem one soul. "None of them can by any means redeem his brother, nor give to God a ransom for him: (for the redemption of their soul is precious)" (Ps. 49:7–8). Why is God alone able to redeem man?

First, God alone has pity enough for man's misery. Boundless misery calls for boundless mercy. But where is such mercy to be found? At most, we find drops among us. But the Creator has infinite mercy for infinite misery and infinite grace for infinite guilt. "As for thy nativity, in the day thou wast born thy naval was not cut, neither wast thou washed in water to supple thee; thou wast not salted at all, nor swaddled at all" (Ezek. 16:4).

Here is misery indeed. What help comes from our fellow man? "None eye pitied thee, to do any of these unto thee, to have compassion upon thee" (v. 5). But what is God's response? "And when I passed by thee, and saw thee polluted in thine own blood, I said unto thee when thou wast in thy blood, Live" (v. 6). God has "great love" for great misery (Eph. 2:4), and "abundant mercy" for abundant misery (1 Peter 1:3). The "tender mercy of our God" has visited us from on high (Luke 1:78).

Second, God alone has wisdom enough to provide a remedy. If God were to offer pardon with the condition that we devise some way to satisfy His infinite justice, we would most certainly perish. We could never find a way to fulfill the law in its commands and curses. We could never think of a way to reconcile God's fury and mercy. We could never have imagined what God has devised. He made the world by His wisdom, and He renews it by His wisdom; hence, His work of redemption reveals His manifold wisdom. In this work is infinite wisdom, because in this work infinite justice and infinite mercy meet (Rom. 3:24–25).

Third, God alone has power enough to secure a recovery. The power of hell must be overcome, the curse of the law must be borne, sin must be subdued, and holiness must be infused. What power can accomplish any of these things? God revealed great power in creating the world out of nothing, but He revealed even greater power in redeeming the world when it was worse than nothing. In the former, He had no opposition; in the latter, the law, devil, and flesh resisted Him. It would have been impossible for our Mediator to endure the power of darkness, the curse of the law, and the fury of His Father without almighty arms underneath Him. "Behold my servant, whom I uphold" (Isa. 42:1). God put forth great power in His work of redemption (Eph. 1:19–20).

God is incomparable not only in what He has done, but also in what He can do. He can do whatever He wills, and He can do more than He wills. His arm is as large as His mind, and His hand is equal to His heart. His pleasure is the only boundary of His strength: "Whatsoever the LORD pleased, that did he in heaven, and in earth, in the seas, and all deep places" (Ps. 135:6). Can we say this of humans or angels? Can we do whatever we please? Surely not, yet God does whatever He pleases: "But he is in one mind, and who can turn him? and what his soul desireth, even that he doeth" (Job 23:13). Only His heart can limit His hand, and only His will can determine His strength. The most powerful people in this world have chains around their hands and feet. They cannot go wherever they please; they can only go wherever God pleases. Likewise, they cannot do whatever they please; they can only do whatever God pleases (Acts 4:27–28).

It is God's prerogative to do whatever He wills. He does not do everything He can but everything He wills. And He can do more than He wills. He "is able to do exceeding abundantly above all that we ask or think" (Eph. 3:20). We can ask for a great number of things, and we can think of more than we can ask. The mind is much larger than the tongue, meaning that our apprehension far exceeds our expression. But God can do "exceeding abundantly" more than we are able to ask or think—so much more that we cannot even think of how much more.

Is anything impossible to God? "For with God nothing shall be impossible" (Luke 1:37). Only God can do everything, as only He can be everything. He is universal in His being and therefore universal in His doing. He can make and unmake worlds in a moment. He can give and take life in the twinkling of an eye. He can build up and tear down. He can stop the sun in its course. Shall the sun go forward or backward ten degrees (2 Kings 20:9–10)? Choose either one—both are easy to God.

CHAPTER 24

God Works Irresistibly

God is also incomparable in the manner of His working. To begin with, He works irresistibly—that is, no one can hinder Him. All the combined power and wisdom of humans and angels cannot stop Him. The mighty Nebuchadnezzar learned this truth while grazing among the wild animals: "He doeth according to his will in the army of heaven, and among the inhabitants of the earth: and none can stay his hand" (Dan. 4:35). God does whatever He wills. "My counsel shall stand, and I will do all my pleasure" (Isa. 46:10). Our counsel does not always stand because God hinders it: "The LORD bringeth the counsel of the heathen to nought: he maketh the devices of the people of none effect" (Ps. 33:10). But we never hinder God's counsel.

God does whatever He wills to do, and there is no hindering Him. If He wills to bring an enemy against a nation, no one can prevent it: "Calling a ravenous bird from the east, the man that executeth my counsel from a far country: yea, I have spoken it, I will also bring it to pass; I have purposed it, I will also do it" (Isa. 46:11). If God wills to deprive people of their estates, treasures, and honors, no one can stop Him: "Behold, he taketh away, who can hinder him?" (Job 9:12). If God wills to remove a kingdom, no one can stand in His way. He removed the four great earthly monarchies. Who opposed Him? All their power could not hinder Him (Dan. 2:44). God controls the motions of all His creatures: "Who is he that saith, and it cometh to pass, when the Lord commandeth it not?" (Lam. 3:37). He "commandeth the sun, and it riseth not; and sealeth up the stars" (Job 9:7). The least light in the sky cannot give light apart from Him.

God does whatever He wills to do, and He never consults with us. As a matter of fact, He challenges us to hinder Him if we can: "I will work, and who shall let it?" (Isa. 43:13). God speaks with all authority. He is above all checks and controls. He challenges us to dare to stand in the way of His motions. He can thwart our greatest attempts and strongest designs: "Take counsel together, and it shall come to nought" (Isa. 8:10). But no one can thwart the least of His attempts: "Behold, he breaketh down, and it cannot be built again; he shutteth up a man, and there can be no opening" (Job 12:14).

CHAPTER 25

God Works Arbitrarily

God works arbitrarily—that is, according to His pleasure. He alone can do whatever He wills. No earthly ruler is absolute or arbitrary in his rule because all rulers are God's subjects and owe allegiance to His majesty and obedience to His commands. But God is absolute and arbitrary, and can do whatever He wills. Everything He does is just, because He does it. "He doeth according to his will in the army of heaven, and among the inhabitants of the earth: and none can stay his hand, or say unto him, What doest thou?" (Dan. 4:35). He is not responsible to anyone for any of His actions. No one can question Him, much less quarrel with Him on account of what He does. He is above all law; therefore, He is above all transgression (1 John 3:4). Because His will is the only rule of rectitude and righteousness, He can do whatever He wills (Rom. 12:2).

He has absolute ownership over the works of His hands, and therefore may dispose of them at His pleasure (Ps. 24:1). We have a civil right to our estates and a natural right to our families, but the original ownership still belongs to God. He divests Himself of nothing by lending or entrusting anything to us. Therefore, He can use what is His according to His pleasure, and no one can question Him for it.

God is supreme and is far above giving an account for anything He does. He is "Most High" (Ps. 92:1). It is no disparagement to humans or angels to be under a law. As a matter of fact, it is essential to us because we are creatures. But God is supreme. He gives all laws to others; therefore He is not under any law. "Why dost thou strive against him? for he giveth not account of any of his matters" (Job 33:13). We often do not strive against God's supremacy with open force but by secret murmuring against His providence. This is vain, for He gives no account of any of His matters. He is not bound to tell us what He does or why He does it. He has received nothing from us; therefore He is not bound to render an account to us (Rom. 11:35).

Who has the authority to call God to account? "Far be it from God, that he should do wickedness; and from the Almighty, that he should commit iniquity.... Who hath given him a charge over the earth? or who hath disposed the whole world?" (Job 34:10, 13). What human? What angel? Where is he? If someone were higher than God and were to give Him a rule, then God would be at fault if He were to swerve from it. But He is higher than the highest of beings; therefore He is His own law. He can do whatever He wills without blame. "Who hath enjoined him his way? or who can say, Thou hast wrought iniquity?" (Job 36:23). God's way is His method of working—His manner of governing the world. Who has any authority over Him to complain about His way of working? It is desperate presumption for any to question God. "Who art thou that repliest against God?" (Rom. 9:20). Who are we? Man is but a clump of clay, piece of dirt, pit of sin, and firebrand of hell. Do we dare contend with our Maker? For shame. Instead, we should sit still and keep silent.

CHAPTER 26

God Works Effortlessly

God works at all times without any weariness. As there is nothing too hard for God, so there is nothing too hard to God. He does the hardest things with ease. Indeed, the great God does the greatest things with the same ease that He does the least things. It is all the same to Him.

The creation was a large building, but God erected it without any effort. The world consists of the celestial and terrestrial globes—both the product of His word: "By the word of the LORD were the heavens made; and all the host of them by the breath of his mouth" (Ps. 33:6). It was but a breath that produced the vast circumference of the heavens with all its luminaries. "For he spake, and it was done; he commanded, and it stood fast" (Ps. 33:9). He spoke the word, and even nonentities obeyed, becoming beings. In the creation account, we see God merely commanding, and immediately all things concurred (Gen. 1:3, 9, 11–12).

In His work of providence, God also does all things effortlessly. He destroys His enemies with the greatest ease. A man crushes a moth between his fingers, but God crushes His enemies with even less effort (Job 4:18–19). He destroys the highest, greatest, and strongest with a breath: "By the blast of God they perish, and by the breath of his nostrils are they consumed" (Job 4:9). It is easy for a man to breathe—to send forth a blast. It is even easier for God, who breathed into man the breath of life. This "blast" does not cause Him any toil or trouble. Sennacherib comes against Jerusalem with a great army, but God deals with him: "Behold, I will send a blast upon him" (2 Kings 19:7). God does not trouble Himself, but simply blows on him. That is all.

God also destroys with a word. If He but speaks, it is done. His saying is doing. "At what instant I shall speak concerning a nation, and concerning a kingdom, to pluck up, and to pull down, and to destroy it" (Jer. 18:7). The prophet declares the certain ruin of the Philistines as follows: "Woe unto the inhabitants of the sea coast…. The word of the LORD is against you" (Zeph. 2:5). That is to say, their condition is desperate, and the world cannot save them, for the "word of the LORD" is against them. People boast a great deal about the things they intend to do, but their words are mere wind. The word of God—like lightning—blasts wherever it goes. God also destroys with a look, with just a glance of His eye. "And it came to pass, that in the morning watch the LORD looked unto the host of the Egyptians through the pillar of fire and of the cloud, and troubled the host of the Egyptians" (Ex. 14:24). One look from God takes away the life of His greatest adversaries.

Moreover, God delivers His people with the greatest ease. Whatever their straits, He helps them. When they are in captivity, He brings them home. "I will say to the north, Give up; and to the south, Keep not back: bring my sons from far, and my daughters from the ends of the earth" (Isa. 43:6). Both north and south heed His word. If He wills it, the work is done. The ocean is a frightful monster. It makes a horrible noise, roaring and raging, as if it would devour us. But God quiets it with ease (Job 38:8–11). The turbulent sea terrified the disciples, yet Christ calmed it effortlessly: "Peace, be still" (Mark 4:39). He spoke like a mother to a crying child. What was the response? "And the wind ceased, and there was a great calm" (v. 39).

CHAPTER 27

God Works Independently

God works entirely by His own power—without the least help from anyone. All creatures are instruments and act in virtue of the principal efficient. That is to say, they act in God's strength. But God alone acts independently. He never requires a helping hand from any of His creatures.

In the work of creation, God erected all things without any instrument: "I am the LORD that maketh all things; that stretcheth forth the heavens alone; that spreadeth abroad the earth by myself" (Isa. 44:24). God made the heavens and earth without any assistance. He says to Job: "Where wast thou when I laid the foundations of the earth? declare, if thou hast understanding" (Job 38:4).

In the work of providence, God does great things on His own: "He stretcheth out the north over the empty place, and hangeth the earth upon nothing" (Job 26:7). He does all things without any help from His creatures. He chooses to use angels and humans in the government of the world. He also chooses to use means such as food, sleep, and medicine for the preservation of our health. But He does not need to use these means. He is the soul of the world, which actuates everything in it. That is why the instruments are called His sword and rod (Ps. 17:13; Isa. 10:5). What can a sword or rod do without a hand to wield them? "Shall the axe boast itself against him that heweth therewith? or shall the saw magnify itself against him that shaketh it?" (Isa. 10:15). The instrument (human or angelic) is but a mere tool in God's hand. We can no more move ourselves than an axe or saw lying on the ground. We dare not speak arrogantly, as if we do everything, when we actually do nothing. God does everything.

Whether God uses means or not, it is all the same to Him. He does as much when He has means as when He has none: "LORD, it is nothing with thee to help, whether with many, or with them that have no power" (2 Chron. 14:11). It does not make the least difference to Him. Whether God has few or many on His side is as insignificant as dust in the balance. God did not make the creatures because He needed them but because it was His pleasure to do so. He uses His creatures because He chooses to use them. In this way, He magnifies His sovereignty, demonstrating His dominion over all His creatures. They are at His beck and call. With a stamp of His foot or a glance of His eye or a whistle of His mouth, He can call them from the uttermost parts of the world to execute His command. "Mine hand also hath laid the foundation of the earth, and my right hand hath spanned the heavens: when I call unto them, they stand up together" (Isa. 48:13).

God can do great things by weak means. He was glorified in Pharaoh by turning pitiful creatures (lice and flies) into plagues (Ex. 8:16–32). God's strength is exceedingly exalted through such poor and weak instruments as humans: "But we have this treasure in earthen vessels, that the excellency of the power may be of God, and not of us" (2 Cor. 4:7). In spiritual things, God works alone—even when He has ministers and ordinances to serve Him. "So then neither is he that planteth any thing, neither he that watereth; but God that giveth the increase" (1 Cor. 3:7). God does not use preachers because they help Him in the conversion of souls. He uses them because it is His pleasure (1 Cor. 1:21). It is often the case that ministers with the greatest gifts are not the most successful in their labor, because God wants us to know that it is not the piety of the preacher but His grace and power which do the work. The preachers are nothing; He is all in all.

It is a great honor to God that He has created millions of creatures, but it is a greater honor to Him that He does not need any of them. They are serviceable to Him, but they are not necessary to Him. God and all His creatures do no more than He can do by Himself.

PART 4

God's Incomparable Words

CHAPTER 28

The Manner of God's Words

God is incomparable in His words. "Behold, God exalt-eth by his power: who teacheth like him?" (Job 36:22). This is a challenge to the whole world. Where is the human or angel who can speak or teach like God? He speaks in an unspeakable manner. This is evident in three prominent ways.

First, God speaks authoritatively. He speaks in His own name. Humans and angels can command, but we do so as subordinates in the name and authority of those over us. But God commands in His own name and authority. He gives authenticity to whatever He speaks, and He speaks with authority when He speaks. He speaks as one who has the right and power to com-mand and as one who (upon His own account) expects to be obeyed. "I am the LORD thy God" (Ex. 20:2). This is enough to warrant obedience. Matthew 7:29 says that Christ "taught them as one having authority, and not as the scribes." He did not request obedience but com-manded it. God is His own authority. We speak from

God, but He speaks from no one but Himself. His word is His "testimony" because it bears witness to itself (Ps. 19:7). We need grounds, reasons, and witnesses to prove what we say to be true. But the Word of God is a sufficient testimony to itself. It is its own proof because what truth speaks must of necessity be true.

Second, God speaks accomodatingly. He speaks to the condition of those whom He addresses. He considers the ability and capacity of His hearers and speaks accordingly. He does not speak in an unknown language (as some ministers do) and exceed the understanding of His hearers; instead, He observes their weaknesses and infirmities—their dullness. He teaches them as they are able to hear. There are depths in His Word where elephants can swim, and there are also shallows where lambs can wade.

In the matter of His teaching, Christ did not give His disciples more than they could grasp: "I have yet many things to say unto you, but ye cannot bear them now" (John 16:12). He had difficult lessons to teach them, but they were young students. They were not able to learn until they had spent more time in His school. Christ did not trouble them but left them to His Spirit, who would enable them to learn the more difficult lessons. Their stomachs still required what was easy to digest—milk, not strong meat (1 Cor. 3:2). Their backs were weak, so He placed only light burdens upon them so that they would not become discouraged.

In the manner of His teaching, Christ was very tender and accommodating. He fit His discourses to His disciples' apprehension: "And with many such parables spake he the word unto them, as they were able to hear it" (Mark 4:33). He did not speak as He was able to speak, but "as they were able to hear." That means He spoke to them in parables so that they might better understand Him. It is true that a parable makes truth more obscure and that speaking in a parable is the opposite of speaking plainly (Ps. 78:2; John 16:25, 29). But a parable—unveiled by Christ—makes truth clearer (Matt. 13:17). It gives the advantage of viewing heavenly truths through earthly glasses. That is why our Savior says, "If I have told you earthly things, and ye believe not, how shall ye believe, if I tell you of heavenly things?" (John 3:12).

Christ's instructions were like water which He poured into those narrow-mouthed vessels little by little—as they were able to receive it. His teaching fell like a gentle rain to refresh them, not as a flood to drown them. Because his children were "tender" and his cattle were "with young," Jacob traveled slowly. He did not want to risk hurting them (Gen. 33:13). Likewise, Christ considers what we are, and He does not drive us too hard. He gives "precept upon precept;…line upon line; here a little, and there a little" (Isa. 28:10). Do we teach with such compassion and accommodation? According to one of the ancients, whoever teaches children must become a child. He must frame and fashion himself to their understanding, or he will never teach them. God demonstrates incomparable patience in condescending to teach us.

Third, God speaks effectually. As He has power to command us, so He has power to enable us to obey. We can tell others their duty, but we cannot force them to observe their duty. We cannot empower them to obey. But God speaks so that His people may hear: "Every man therefore that hath heard, and hath learned of the Father, cometh unto me" (John 6:45). Some people are so dull that no one can teach them. But God can make the dull, blind, and ignorant to consider, apprehend, and understand the most difficult things (Isa. 32:4). His power accompanies His speaking. When He says, "Let there be light," there is light in a dark mind. He commands "the light to shine out of darkness" (2 Cor. 4:6). When He says, "Let there be life," there is life in a dead soul (John 5:24). We can command the blind to see and the dead to live over and over again, but it is all in vain. Yet if God says to a sinner who lies in the grave, rotting from the vermin of his lusts, stinking in the sight of others, languishing in the devil's chains, "Sinner, come forth," he comes forth to live forever.

The disciples said of Christ: "What manner of man is this, that even the winds and the sea obey him!" (Matt. 8:27). Even so, we may say, "Oh what manner of God is this, that even the high winds of violent passions and the fierce waves of boisterous corruptions obey Him!" They fall before Him. Can we speak like this? Does sin die at our word? Does the soul live at our command? If God speaks, the most obstinate sinner obeys His voice, submits to His will, and yields to His word. When God speaks, even demons must leave their beloved mansions—the souls of men (Matt. 8:32). If God says, "Get thee hence, Satan," the prince of the power of the air and the god of this world sneaks away like a coward (Matt. 4:10–11). With a mere word, God ejects Satan out of his strongest hold—the souls of seared and senseless sinners. He leads captivity captive, making this jailer His prisoner (Eph. 4:8).

CHAPTER 29

The Matter of God's Words

In addition to the manner of His speech, God is also incomparable in the matter of His speech. This incomparability is evident in several features of God's Word. The first is the purity of its precepts. It is the most perfect rule of righteousness that is imaginable. It commands all good and forbids all evil at all times. "Wherefore the law is holy, and the commandment holy, and just, and good" (Rom. 7:12). It is holy because it is a copy of the divine will, it is just because it corresponds to the highest reason, and it is good because it is most beneficial to us. It is holy as it relates to our duty to God, it is just as it respects our duty to our neighbor, and it is good as it concerns our duty to ourselves. It is holy as consecrated to the service of God, it is just as a transcript of the law of nature, and it is good as it is the measure of all goodness in us. It is holy in what it requires us to do, it is just in what it forbids us to do, and it is good in both. What law in the world is in any degree comparable to God's law?

It is so pure that there is not the slightest error in it. It commands conformity to the mind of the great Sovereign of all things. It is so perfect that it is not deficient in anything (Ps. 19:7). It commands purity in the whole man—in every faculty of the soul and in every member of the body. It commands purity at all times and in all companies, conditions, relations, and circumstances (Ps. 119:1–2; 1 Peter 1:15–16). It is apparent to common sense that we could never have invented such a law. We are so far from it and so completely contrary to it (Rom. 8:7). Angels could not have imagined it unless God had revealed His mind to them. All holiness is conformity to the will of the most high God; therefore, angels could not have discerned what was holy and unholy any more than they could have discovered the will of this incomparable God.

The second feature of God's incomparable Word is the mystery of its doctrines. It acquaints us with things far above our reach. "O the depth of the riches both of the wisdom and knowledge of God!" (Rom. 11:33). God's Word contains a depth that no one can fathom. Who could have imagined that a woman could be both virgin and mother? Who could have imagined that millions of people would be members of one body, living wholly by one Head (Eph. 5:27–30; Col. 2:19)? Who could have imagined that three distinct persons would be one in nature and essence? Who could have imagined that God would become man, or that He who made all things would be born of a woman? Who could have imagined that the Bread of Life would be hungry, the Water of Life would be thirsty, the only Rest would be weary, and the only Joy would be sorrowful? Who could have imagined that millions would be enriched by another's poverty, filled by another's emptiness, exalted by another's disgrace, healed by another's wounds, eased by another's pains, and absolved by another's condemnation? Who could have imagined that infinite justice and infinite mercy would be made friends at the cross? Who could have imagined that the greatest fury and greatest favor, the greatest hatred and greatest love would be manifested in Christ's death? Could we have invented such mysteries?

The third feature of God's incomparable Word is the certainty of its prophecies. We cannot foretell things that are independent of natural causes—but God can, and He never fails in His predictions. He foretells the birth of Cyrus one hundred years beforehand (Isa. 44:28), the birth of Josiah two hundred years beforehand (1 Kings 13:2), and the conversion of the Gentiles two thousand years beforehand (Gen. 9:27; Isa. 49:6). He foretells the birth of Christ close to four thousand years before He came into the world (Gen. 3:15). And He provides specific details concerning Christ's advent: He predicts His tribe (Judah) and family (David); He tells of His virgin birth; He speaks of the place of His birth (Bethlehem) and the place of His sojourn (Egypt);

He indicates that He will be reviled, disgraced, tempted, betrayed, arrested, deserted, pierced, and buried; He reveals that He will rise again and reap the fruit of all His passion to His full satisfaction.

Can any human or angel foretell such things? God challenges all so-called gods: "Shew the things that are to come hereafter, that we may know that ye are gods" (Isa. 41:23). The certain prediction of future events is such a prerogative of deity that God promises to acknowledge the supremacy and sovereignty of whoever can do it. Foreknowledge is a jewel in God's crown that no one has ever shared: "I have declared the former things from the beginning; and they went forth out of my mouth, and I shewed them; I did them suddenly, and they came to pass.... I have even from the beginning declared it to thee; before it came to pass, I shewed it thee" (Isa. 48:3, 5). God alone foreknows and foretells whatever comes to pass. "Known unto God are all his works from the beginning of the world" (Acts 15:18). He stands on the high mountain of eternity and has a full view of all that His will produces.

CHAPTER 30

The Effect of God's Words

God's words are His works. They accomplish His purposes while also declaring His pleasure. They possess both power and virtue. God's Word can stop the tide of nature when it flows with the greatest violence, actually turning it in the opposite direction. Imagine a man who is in the height of his strength and in the passions of his youth. He is drinking a large draught of carnal pleasures and enjoying a full gust of sensual delights, making his life but a diversion from one pleasure to another. This man is in his best estate, the zenith of health and strength, and the meridian of his age. He convinces himself that he will live a long life, thereby giving himself the more liberty to indulge his lusts. But if God's Word comes to this man, it will make him forsake his foolish pleasures, leave his beloved lusts, and loathe himself for having loved them. It will alter his palate—what was sweet will become bitter and what was bitter will become sweet. It will change the frame of his heart; he will forsake what he previously viewed as his only happiness.

We can attempt to persuade others, but God alone can prevail. Our words can provoke outward reformation, but only God's Word can produce inward renovation. He alone made the heart, and He alone can mend it. Human counsel can do something to hide the corruption of nature, but only divine instruction is effectual for the healing of corrupted nature. "The law of the LORD is perfect, converting the soul" (Ps. 19:7). The law of man can bind the body to good behavior, but only the law of God can bring the soul to good behavior. God's Word alone can turn a lion into a lamb, darkness into light, and death into life (Isa. 11:6–8; Eph. 2:1, 5; 5:8).

God speaks—not as humans or angels to the ears alone, but to the heart, shattering it in pieces. He aims His threats and terrors at the conscience, leveling it to the ground. When God speaks, He strikes fear into people (Ex. 19:19; Heb. 12:21). "The voice of the LORD is powerful; the voice of the LORD is full of majesty. The voice of the LORD breaketh the cedars; yea, the LORD breaketh the cedars of Lebanon" (Ps. 29:4–5). By the Word, the obstinate and ignorant are terrified in their soul, wounded in their conscience, and forced to cry, "What shall we do?" (Acts 2:37). When God speaks, the most stubborn and senseless sinner falls to the ground with the very fire of hell flaming in his conscience. God's Word strikes his heart like an arrow in the side of a buck. In the night, He terrifies him with dreams and visions. In the day, He does not give him any rest, forcing him to carry his tormented conscience wherever he goes.

Who knows the power of God's anger (Ps. 90:11)? Who is able to fear Him according to His wrath? "Hast thou an arm like God? or canst thou thunder with a voice like him?" (Job 40:9). If He utters a word of fury, the rocks are torn in pieces; the stony heart is melted; the mountains are moved; the greatest sinner is humbled; and the foundations of the world are shaken—the whole frame of nature is troubled.

When God takes the sword of the Spirit in His hand, it wounds in the conscience: it awakens the sleepy soul; it frightens the secure soul; and it affects the senseless soul with its sin and misery (Acts 2:37). We taste the bitterness of original and actual corruption: "For mine iniquities are gone over mine head: as a heavy burden they are too heavy for me" (Ps. 38:4). We feel the weight of divine indignation. The unquenchable fire flashes in our face. In this condition, we do not know what to do, for "a wounded spirit who can bear?" (Prov. 18:14). We turn to others, but they are unable to provide any help. They are useless comforters. Only the hand that wounded can heal.

> Fools because of their transgression, and because of their iniquities, are afflicted. Their soul abhorreth all manner of meat; and they draw near unto the gates of death. Then they cry unto the LORD in their trouble, and he saveth them out of their

distresses. He sent his word, and healed them,
and delivered them from their destructions.
(Ps. 107:17–20)

Friends, ministers, and angels can speak, but it
is all in vain. Their words cannot cure these wounds.
But if God is pleased to speak, the dying soul revives.
His Word is the only balm that can cure the wounded
conscience: "He sent his word, and healed them." Conscience is God's prisoner; He claps it in chains through
His Word. The world cannot open the door, break the
chains, and release the prisoner. Only He who shut it in
can let it out.

David professed that he would have fainted if it
had not been for God's Word: "Unless thy law had
been my delights, I should then have perished in mine
affliction" (Ps. 119:92). He would have sunk in the deep
waters of affliction without God's Word to support and
sustain him.

PART 5

Application

CHAPTER 31

The Malignity of Sin

We arrive at the application of this great doctrine: God is incomparable. In the first place, God's incomparable nature informs us of sin's malignity. Sin is an injury to the great and glorious God. The better the object is, the baser the action that injures it. Throwing dirt on old rags is not as bad as throwing dirt on new garments. Making a flaw in a common stone is not as bad as making a flaw in a precious stone. The object's worth heightens and aggravates the offense. How horrid then is sin! It does not oppose rulers (the highest of humans) or angels (the highest of creatures), but God (the highest of beings). He is the incomparable God, in comparison to whom the whole creation is less than nothing.

We perceive the size of sin to be too small when we only measure it by the wrong it does to us, our families, or our neighbors. Indeed, we see something of its evil in its effect upon these things, but we only perceive its full size when we consider the wrong it does to the incomparable God. Sin is incomparably malignant because the God principally injured by it is incomparably excellent. It is one thing to offend a man—a mere creature. It is another thing to offend God—an incomparably immense being. "If one man sin against another, the judge shall judge him: but if a man sin against the LORD, who shall intreat for him?" (1 Sam. 2:25). Here we have a finite creature (man) offending the infinite Creator. Who dares to arbitrate for man? Who dares to intercede for him? There is an infinite demerit in sin because it is an injury to an infinite majesty. Nothing reveals sin to be so great an evil as its opposition to so great, so matchless, and so incomparable a God. This is the only mirror that shows the horrid features and monstrous deformities of sin's face. It is an affront to the blessed God—"the high and lofty One" (Isa. 57:15).

To sin is to disobey the incomparable God. It is a breach of His law—a violation of His command and a contradiction of His will. "Whosoever committeth sin transgresseth also the law: for sin is the transgression of the law" (1 John 3:4). The size of our obedience or disobedience is not determined by the size of the thing commanded or forbidden, nor by the size of the good or hurt done, but by the greatness of God, who commands or forbids.

To sin is to disdain the incomparable God. It is contempt for His authority. It is to slight His dominion and deny His sovereignty. This is the voice of every sinner: "Who is the LORD, that I should obey his voice?"

(Ex. 5:2). They know no maker and therefore own no master. For this reason, sinners cast the incomparable God behind their back, as not worth acknowledging (1 Kings 14:9).

To sin is to dishonor the incomparable God. If it is unacceptable to reproach our fellow man, how bad is it to reproach the great God? Sin lays the honor of this incomparable God in the dust and tramples on it. Sin degrades and dethrones God. It will not allow Him to be Lord of the world. It defaces His image wherever it is found. Sin disgraces His justice; hence it is unrighteousness (1 John 1:9). Sin disgraces His wisdom; hence it is foolishness (Prov. 5:23). It disgraces His patience; hence it is murmuring (Jude 16). It disgraces His power; hence it is weakness (Rom. 5:6). It disgraces His mercy; hence it is ingratitude (Luke 6:35). It disgraces His knowledge; hence it is ignorance (1 Peter 1:14). It disgraces His truth; hence it is wickedness (Ps. 58:2). In each of these ways, sin disgraces God's holiness, which is His glory (Ex. 15:11).

To sin is to destroy the incomparable God. The murder of any person is horrid (Gen. 4:10; Matt. 10:28). The murder of a parent or ruler is even more heinous. But what a monster is that person who destroys (as far as he is able) the good, great, gracious, glorious, and incomparable God! Truly, sin is such a monster, such a devil, that were its power equal to its spite and its strength answerable to its malice, the living God would not live a moment. All sin is God-murder. The sinner hates God (Rom. 1:30), and hate always seeks the destruction of its object. "The fool hath said in his heart, There is no God" (Ps. 14:1). It pleases him to think there is no God. He is like a guilty prisoner who likes to imagine there is no judge to condemn him. We hate whatever we perceive as hurtful to us. Consequently, we wish it were taken out of the way. In the same way, the sinner strives and contends with God. He fights against Him. "For he stretcheth out his hand against God, and strengtheneth himself against the Almighty" (Job 15:25). In other words, he attacks God as an enemy.

Oh how odious, loathsome, and abominable is sin! It breaks the law, slights the authority, dishonors the name, and seeks to destroy the being of this incomparable God—this self-sufficient, independent, perfect, eternal, incomprehensible, infinite being! Imagine if this God were to appear to you and show you but a glimpse of His excellent glory—that greatness which the heavens cannot contain; that duration which has no beginning, succession, or end; that boundless and limitless perfection which is incapable of the least addition or accession—and then say to you (as He said to Saul), "Why persecutest thou me?" (Acts 9:4). What would you then think of your sin?

Should we not think differently about our sin? Should we not loathe ourselves for being so unworthy— yea, so mad—as to fight against such a God? Should we not cry out with Job: "I have sinned; what shall I do unto thee, O thou preserver of men?" (Job 7:20). We have sinned against an incomparable, infinite, and inconceivable being. We have wronged the most high, most holy, and most blessed God. What amends can we make? It is impossible for us to make the least satisfaction for the injury done to His majesty. We should cry out with Job: "I have heard of thee by the hearing of the ear: but now mine eye seeth thee. Wherefore I abhor myself, and repent in dust and ashes" (Job 42:5–6). We have heard of God through His Word and works. They have told us something of His beauty, glory, and excellency. We have seen something of His majesty, royalty, and sovereignty. Should we not abhor ourselves for transgressing His will, blaspheming His name, despising His supremacy, and fighting against His majesty? Should we not loathe ourselves for daring to contend with His excellency? Should we not repent, grieving for our sin? Should we not lie in the dust, acknowledging that we are lower than the dust?

This is the malignity of sin. It is contrary, offensive, and injurious to the incomparable God. This consideration should humble us. This was the weight that crushed David: "Against thee, thee only, have I sinned, and done this evil in thy sight" (Ps. 51:4). David had sinned against God's enemies by encouraging their blasphemy, against God's friends by grieving their spirits, against his kingdom by provoking God, against Bathsheba by defiling her, and against Uriah by defrauding him of his wife and life. Yet David looks upon these (although great sins in themselves) as nothing in comparison to his sin against God. The arrow that pierced his heart was this: "I have sinned against the LORD" (2 Sam. 12:13). This is the weightiest argument to drive us from sin.

CHAPTER 32

The Madness of Sinners

If God is incomparable, sinners who dare to offend Him to His face must be entirely mad. If we were to see a man (without any cause) striving against an army of soldiers, provoking them to kill him, we would think he was mad. Why else would he lead himself to certain ruin? Every time we willfully break God's laws, we act like a madman. We fight against God, who is stronger than millions of armies. We provoke the Almighty, who is able to wink us into hell.

Are we any match for God? "Do we provoke the Lord to jealousy? are we stronger than he?" (1 Cor. 10:22). It is one thing to provoke a person to anger, but it is another thing to provoke God to anger. A man has a small heart and small hands—his anger and power are finite. But God's heart and hands (His anger and power) are infinite. If the king's wrath is a messenger of death, then what is the wrath of omnipotence? Do we realize what we do when we break God's law, slight His love, dishonor His name, and grieve His Spirit? We provoke

God, who has threatened to destroy us. He is incomparable in power, and He can accomplish what He has threatened. He is incomparable in truth, and He will fulfill what He has threatened. "Woe unto him that striveth with his Maker!" (Isa. 45:9). If we insist on striving, then we should meddle with our equals—not our Maker. He is infinitely superior to us in power and authority. This is impudence indeed: a pitiful nothing challenging the Almighty. "Who would set the briers and thorns against me in battle? I would go through them, I would burn them together" (Isa. 27:4). Briers and thorns are no match for fire. How easily, speedily, and certainly does fire consume them! Weak men are no match for God, who is a consuming fire! What leader, before going to war, does not first determine whether his thousand men are able to contend with his enemy's fifty thousand men? Does he not decide to seek peace rather than fight?

How great the madness of those who will risk the eternal loss of this incomparable God! According to Christ, the person who risks the loss of the incomparable God for a little corruptible gold is a fool (Luke 12:20). The prodigal son was out of his mind when he left the bread of his father's house for husks in the pigs' pen (Luke 15:18–20). When he came to his senses, he realized how foolish he was to wallow among swine when he could feast at his father's table.

We must think of this the next time we are tempted to sin. Will this moment's pleasure compensate for the loss of God, who is eternal life—a river of unimaginable and unchangeable pleasures? Will we be so bewitched as to lose real mercies for lying vanities; the fountain of living waters for broken cisterns; the food of angels for the world's scraps; a precious soul, inestimable Savior, and incomparable God for a toy and trifle? Did anyone ever buy so dear or sell so cheap or manifest such madness?

CHAPTER 33

The Misery of Sinners

The misery of sinners consists in the fact that they will depart from the incomparable God for all eternity. "Depart from me, ye that work iniquity" (Matt. 7:23). "Depart from me, ye cursed" (Matt. 25:41). What a dreadful sound will the word "depart" make in sinners' ears! What a deep wound will it make in their hearts! They will lose their earthly riches, honors, and comforts. They will lose their health, family, and friends. They will lose the communion of perfect saints, the company of glorious angels, and the blessed exercises of the heavenly host. Far eclipsing these, they will depart from the incomparable God forever. They will lose the only Paradise of pleasure, the only Fountain of living water, and the only Author of true happiness. They will lose the unsearchable Mine of riches, the inexhaustible Well of salvation, and the inestimable Sun of righteousness. They will lose the dearest Father, wisest Guide, strongest Shield, sweetest Love, closest Friend, richest Grace, and highest Honor. They will lose the Lord of life, Lord of glory, Lord of Lords, God of hope, God of all grace, God of all comfort, God of peace, God of gods, and God and Father of our Lord Jesus Christ. They will lose Him totally and finally. This is the loss of all losses. It is a loss that no tongue can declare and no mind can comprehend. There has never been a loss like it. He who loses God loses all that is worth having: "Lord, to whom shall we go? thou hast the words of eternal life" (John 6:68).

How great is the sinner's loss in the other world, whatever his gain in this world! Can the greatest gain in this world compensate for the loss of God? The greatness of any loss is measured by the value of what is lost. If God is incomparable, then the loss of Him must be incomparable. As there is no gain equal to the gain of God, so there is no loss equal to the loss of God. All other losses pale in comparison. All that is good is gone forever. In the other world, the sinner will be wholly ruined and utterly undone. He loses God, and with Him all that is good.

If you live without God, consider what you are missing. Do you not think it will fill your heart with anguish to hear the blessed God say to you, "Depart from Me"? Those words will sound more miserably in your ears than you can conceive at present. They will mark the end of all your joys, hopes, comforts, and delights. They will announce the end of whatever is refreshing and reviving to you at present—all your ease, rest, peace, health, strength, friends, and all that affords a little comfort and happiness.

Perhaps you think you can be happy without God. Perhaps you even say to Him: "Depart from us; for we desire not the knowledge of thy ways" (Job 21:14). The reason for your atheism and profanity is your ignorance. You do not realize that God is a fountain of life, mine of love, hive of sweetness, and ocean of happiness. When you enter the other world, you will know it. You will know what you have lost. At that moment, you will believe the truth of Scripture in all its revelations. But, to your terror and torment, your faith will be that of a demon. You will see that you have lost God, who is a vast treasure, perfect good, and river of pleasure. You will see that you have lost perfect joy, solid comfort, real satisfaction, and eternal glory. You will understand that you have lost all this on account of your lusts, your foolish temporal pleasures. At that moment, what thoughts will fill your mind? What anguish and remorse will overwhelm you? You will curse yourself for your madness. You will gnash your teeth out of envy toward those who sit at heaven's table, feasting on the fruit from the Tree of Life, and drinking from the pure rivers of water which flow from God's throne. You will wail on account of your negligence—that you refused the offer of all these things, shutting the door of heaven and happiness with your own hands.

At present, you know very little of what it means to lose the incomparable God. I assure you that all joy and comfort disappear with this one word: "Depart." It will mark the end of every bit of bread, drop of water, glimpse of light, and crumb of comfort.

In addition to their departure from God, the misery of sinners arises from the fact that God will be their eternal enemy: "Woe also to them when I depart from them!" (Hos. 9:12). Since there is no friend like God, their lack of His friendship is inconceivably great. And since there is no enemy like God, their misery is beyond comparison. The greater the power and anger, the greater the misery of those who fall under the stroke of that power and anger. God is incomparable in anger. His anger roots up, pulls down, kills, slaughters, removes mountains, and shakes the foundations of the earth. He is a consuming fire, burning all that comes near. "Thou, even thou, art to be feared: and who may stand in thy sight when once thou art angry?" (Ps. 76:7). Woe to those who have this God as their enemy! "It is a fearful thing to fall into the hands of the living God" (Heb. 10:31).

After death, sinners are the object of God's wrath. He puts away all compassion and tenderness. The other world is the place where His justice (which is presently clouded and eclipsed) shines forth in full strength. It appears in all its beauty and brightness. It will be terrifying for a mere creature to fall into the hands of the living God with nothing but his own soul to bear the stroke of infinite anger. Sinners will be unable to escape or endure the weight of His omnipotent arm and infinite anger. Take it to heart, and make your peace with Him through His Son. Why would you, for a little profit and pleasure for a few days, risk boiling in the furnace of the almighty God's anger forever? Friend, be wise!

CHAPTER 34

The Folly of Pride

If God is incomparable, those who prefer themselves above God are guilty of abominable pride and presumption. If He is so transcendently excellent in His being, attributes, works, and words, then how desperately impudent are those who put themselves in the balance with God! "All nations before him are as nothing; and they are counted to him less than nothing, and vanity. To whom then will ye liken God? or what likeness will ye compare unto him?" (Isa. 40:17–18). To liken God to anything is the grossest idolatry, and to liken anything to God is the highest arrogance.

It is debasing to God when we fail to adore and admire Him according to His excellent majesty. It is even more debasing to God when we compare Him with poor pitiful nothings—as all humans and angels are in relation to Him. He humbles Himself to look upon humans and angels, "to behold the things that are in heaven, and in the earth" (Ps. 113:6). But He will not debase Himself by being compared with humans and angels. He is infinitely above and beyond all comparatives and superlatives.

Can we compare the clay with the potter? The potter would think it a great dishonor to be compared to the clay. He has a heaven-born spiritual and immortal soul. It would be sheer arrogance on the part of the clay to compare itself with the potter. Is it not even greater pride for humans or angels to compare themselves with God when there is such an infinite distance between them? Yet they are so arrogant that they dare to do this very thing. Both aspired to be equal with their Maker. Both desired to be independent and self-sufficient. Both endeavored to cut off God. By aspiring to raise themselves, they actually ruined themselves and made themselves baser than beasts.

It is a great privilege that humans and angels can be like God in some rays and beams of His purity and holiness. But it is impossible for them to be like God in the rich jewels of His crown: independence, perfection, infiniteness, and supremacy. He stamped some impressions of Himself upon His creatures, but He took no impressions of His creatures upon Himself. He made them in His likeness, but He was not made in their likeness. It is devilish blasphemy for the highest creature to weigh himself against the Creator. This was Lucifer's pride: "I will ascend into heaven, I will exalt my throne above the stars of God...I will be like the Most High" (Isa. 14:13–14). But his pride resulted in his fall. God cannot tolerate a rival. There is but one sun in the heavens. A human king might take it kindly if his subjects endeavor to imitate him in his mercy, justice, temperance, charity, and other characteristics. They acknowledge excellence in him by imitating him. But if his subjects attempt to imitate him in his regalia (those things that are proper to him as a king such as making laws, wearing the crown, and ascending the throne), he will judge them as rebels. Likewise, God is pleased that humans and angels should resemble Him in those perfections that are common and communicable—patience, righteousness, and holiness—thereby glorifying Him (Matt. 5:16). But if His creatures seek to be like Him in the prerogatives of His deity (independence, sovereignty, etc.), He will not suffer it, for they attempt to dethrone Him.

How often does God tell us to quell such presumptuous thoughts? "I am God, and not man" (Hos. 11:9). "God is not a man" (Num. 23:19). As Job declares, "He is not a man, as I am" (Job 9:32). God was pleased (out of His infinite goodness) to become man, so that man might once more be like Him in His communicable properties, but He will not permit man to become God—that is, to be like Him in the special prerogatives of His deity. There is an infinite distance between the divine and human natures. Those who talk about being turned into the essence of deity (as some have impudently and blasphemously written) are either intolerably weak or devilishly wicked.

Many people are guilty of presuming to compare themselves with God. I will mention but a few sorts. First, there are those who quarrel with God's precepts, as if they were too pure and precise. In doing so, they prefer themselves before God. They speak as if they were seated on God's throne, making laws. Because man has corrupted his nature, he is angry at God for restricting and forbidding that which feeds his disease.

Second, there are those who question God's providence, as if it were not good, wise, and righteous. They too prefer themselves before God. Their voice is like Absalom's: "Oh that I were made judge in the land" (2 Sam. 15:4). They think that if they governed the world, there would not be as much disorder among us—the righteous would not perish and the wicked would not flourish. In thinking like this, they contend with God for sovereignty: "Why dost thou strive against him?" (Job 33:13). They accuse God of folly and think they are wiser: "Shall he that contendeth with the Almighty instruct him?" (Job 40:2). Whoever complains of God's providence seeks to teach God how the world should be governed. They condemn God as unjust: "Wilt thou condemn me, that thou mayest be righteous?" (Job 40:8). God's ways are often secret; His paths are in the "great waters" (Ps. 77:19). Because people cannot fathom His ways, they find fault with them. God writes His mind in dark characters. Because poor, blind men cannot read them, they wrangle with them: "Thy judgments are a great deep" (Ps. 36:6).

Third, there are those who complain of God's decrees, as if they were partial and unrighteous. They think that if they had been present at heaven's council table when all was determined, the conclusions would have been more just and righteous. They think and speak evil of things they do not understand. Their time would be better spent considering faith and repentance and ensuring their effectual calling rather than prying into heaven's secrets. No one has a line long enough to measure God. His eternal works and ways are beyond our understanding. They merit our admiration rather than our presumptuous disputation (Rom. 9:17–24).

CHAPTER 35

The Importance of Worship

If God is incomparable, then He deserves incomparable worship. Solomon gives the following reason why the temple had to be great: "For great is our God above all gods" (2 Chron. 2:5). God is great; therefore our worship of Him must be great. God is the best; therefore our service to Him must be the best. It reflects poorly upon God when we give something ordinary to Him. "But cursed be the deceiver, which hath in his flock a male, and voweth, and sacrificeth unto the Lord a corrupt thing" (Mal. 1:14). Why is the quality of the sacrifice so important? God is "a great King," and His name is "dreadful among the heathen." A great sovereign must have great sacrifices.

First, God's excellency calls for incomparable reverence. "Shall not his excellency make you afraid? and his dread fall upon you?" (Job 13:11). Great distance calls for great reverence. There is a great civil distance between masters and servants; therefore servants must obey their masters "with fear and trembling" (Eph. 6:5).

Now, there is an infinite distance between God and us; therefore there ought to be (if it were possible) infinite reverence. Should not the vastness of His perfections provoke us to awe? He is so far above all others in excellency that He alone deserves the name of excellency (Ps. 111:9). "For the LORD is great, and greatly to be praised: he is to be feared above all gods" (Ps. 96:4). Surely, we must seek to be "in the fear of the LORD all the day long" (Prov. 23:17). This is particularly true when we appear before Him. How should we appear before the One who inhabits eternity? "Keep thy foot when thou goest to the house of God, and be more ready to hear, than to give the sacrifice of fools: for they consider not that they do evil. Be not rash with thy mouth, and let not thine heart be hasty to utter any thing before God: for God is in heaven, and thou upon earth" (Eccl. 5:1–2). God is "clothed with majesty" (Ps. 93:1); therefore we must be filled with awe.

Second, God's excellency calls for incomparable humility. When we compare ourselves to those who have little, we are puffed up with pride, but when we see ourselves in the light of the incomparable God, we abhor ourselves for our pride. We never come to a right knowledge of ourselves (what pitiful and abominable wretches we are), until we come to a right knowledge of God (what an excellent and incomparable majesty He is). When people look down on those who are below them, they swim in their conceit. They think they are somebody. But when they look up to the great God (the substance of all excellency), their high-mindedness evaporates. Upon seeing the incomparable God, the most excellent person loathes (rather than admires) himself. When Isaiah saw the God of glory sitting on His throne, encircled with millions of celestial courtiers covering their faces, crying, "Holy, holy, holy," what did he think of himself? "Woe is me! for I am undone; because I am a man of unclean lips…for mine eyes have seen the King, the LORD of hosts" (Isa. 6:5). Isaiah saw himself as a pitiful creature.

Third, God's excellency calls for incomparable love. Love is the cream of our affections. Its object is goodness; therefore the greater the good, the greater our love. Since God is the greatest good, He deserves our greatest love. "Thou shalt love the Lord thy God with all thy heart, and with all thy soul, and with all thy mind" (Matt. 22:37). This is the greatest commandment—all the commandments in one (Rom. 13:10). As the greatest perfection, God must have the greatest affection. He deserves the greatest extensively: the heart, soul, and mind. And He deserves the greatest intensively: all the heart, all the soul, and all the mind. Our love for God must be so great that our love for our father, mother, spouse, children, house, land, and life is hatred in comparison (Luke 14:26). There is nothing worthy of our love like God, and there is nothing worthy of our love besides God. All our friends, relations, and possessions are instruments for His glory. All sacraments and seasons of grace are only lovely in so far as they are means of communion with His majesty: "LORD, I have loved the habitation of thy house, and the place where thine honor dwelleth" (Ps. 26:8).

Desire and delight are the two acts of love, distinguished only by the absence or presence of the object. When the object of love is absent, the soul desires it. When the object of love is present, the soul delights in it. The former is the soul's motion, whereas the latter is the soul's rest. Now, the incomparable God must have incomparable desires: panting, longing, and fainting (Pss. 42:1; 119:20, 40, 81). We must desire Him above all: "Whom have I in heaven but thee? and there is none upon earth that I desire beside thee" (Ps. 73:25). The incomparable God must also have incomparable delight: "Then will I go unto the altar of God, unto God my exceeding joy" (Ps. 43:4). Our souls must be ravished in the enjoyment of God (Song 2:4).

Fourth, God's excellency calls for incomparable trust. The more powerful and faithful a person is, the more firmly we trust him. God is incomparable in power and faithfulness; therefore He deserves our surest love and firmest faith (Rom. 4:20; Heb. 6:18). We must esteem His words as good as deeds, and we must rely on all His promises as if they were already fulfilled. We rejoice in hope of the good things promised as if we already possessed them (Rom. 5:1–5).

Fifth, God's excellency calls for incomparable obedience. The more virtuous and honorable a person is, the more we watch ourselves in his presence. God is incomparable in purity and majesty; therefore we must not walk carelessly but carefully (Eph. 5:15). We do not merely obey at some seasons and in some actions, but at all times and in all things. "But as he which hath called you is holy, so be ye holy in all manner of conversation" (1 Peter 1:15). Our obedience must be incomparable because partial obedience is unsuitable to such a great God.

CHAPTER 36

The Wonder of Grace

If God is incomparable, then His grace is infinite. Oh that the God of heaven should show goodness to those who are rebels against His majesty! David declares, "O LORD our Lord, how excellent is thy name in all the earth! who hast set thy glory above the heavens.... What is man, that thou art mindful of him? and the son of man, that thou visitest him?" (Ps. 8:1, 4). What grace that God minds a poor, silly, simple man; a weak, frail, dying man; a sinful, filthy, polluted man; a lost, wretched, miserable man! This is cause for admiration and astonishment. "What is man, that thou art mindful of him?" We are not worthy to occupy even a moment in God's mind. "And the son of man, that thou visitest him?" We do not deserve anything from the beasts of the earth, much less the angels of heaven—and least of all the God of heaven. What a wonder that the God of heaven should do so much for our good!

God manifests wondrous grace in taking care of our temporal concerns. We would think it a great grace for a human king to take care of a poor beggar: to provide him with food, shelter, medicine, and safety; to supply him in all his needs, support him in all his weaknesses, protect him in all his dangers, and deliver him in all his distresses; to spread his table, provide his food, clothe his body, and make his bed; to protect him, counsel him, and assist him. The King of kings (to whom all earthly kings are but dirt and dung) does more than this! He sends us food, shelter, and clothing and makes them refreshing to us. He is with us in our goings and comings—to keep us alive, enable us in our motions, relieve us in our needs, and defend us from all our adversaries. Is not His condescension worthy of all admiration? Oh what grace that the incomparable God (who has millions of glorious angels serving Him) should serve poor worms!

This incomparable God manifests even greater grace in His care of our precious souls. Here He shows "the exceeding riches of his grace" (Eph. 2:7). Is it not grace in the highest degree for this perfect, self-sufficient, incomparable God to look on us? When we were naked, restless, famished, wallowing in blood, gasping for breath, waiting for demons to escort us to the dungeon of darkness, God looked on us with favor. He clothed us with His righteousness and satisfied us with flesh that is meat indeed and blood that is drink indeed. He gave us rest in His bosom. He bound our wounds, raised us from the dead, and freed us from bondage to Satan, sin, death, and hell. He adopted us as His children, accepted us as righteous, married us to His only begotten Son, and made us heirs of all things. He dwells in us by His Spirit, carries us on eagle's wings, leads us through the wilderness of the world, and brings us to a heavenly Canaan—to fullness of joy, rivers of pleasure, crowns of life, and weights of glory. There, we will reign in His incomparable majesty for all eternity.

What grace is this! The incomparable God has no obligation to us, and He has no need of us. He does not receive anything from us. Moreover, He has all the reason in the world to destroy us. Yet He is pleased to be as studious and solicitous of our welfare as if it were His own. Is it not a wonder that the incomparable God should wed us to Himself? David admired that God would do so much for him. "Who am I, O Lord GOD? and what is my house, that thou hast brought me hitherto? And this was yet a small thing in thy sight, O Lord GOD; but thou hast spoken also of thy servant's house for a great while to come" (2 Sam. 7:18–19). Do we not have cause to say the same?

This grace is even more admirable when we consider the means by which this incomparable God accomplished our recovery. He became a weak, weary, hungry, contemptible man. The Lord of All became a servant, the Lord of Glory became of no reputation, the Bread of Life was hungry, the only Blessing was made a curse, and the Prince of Life was put to death. The angels pry into this deep mystery with such astonishing pleasure. This is marvelous grace "which passeth knowledge" (Eph. 3:19).

CHAPTER 37

Knowing God

The doctrine of God's incomparableness is also useful by way of counsel. To begin with, we must study the knowledge of this God. We count it a privilege to know people who are eminent and excellent in position, power, and piety. It is in our interest to make their acquaintance. If we were to hear of someone as strong as Samson, who could kill hundreds with a jawbone; or someone as old as Methuselah, who could tell of events from thousands of years ago; or someone as wise as Solomon, who could answer the most difficult questions, we would pay a high price to make their acquaintance. But what are such people in comparison to the blessed God? They are but pitiful nothings. What is Samson's strength in comparison to the power of Almighty God? It is chaff in the wind. What is Methuselah's age in comparison to the duration of the eternal God? It is a "handbreadth" (Ps. 39:5). What is Solomon's wisdom in comparison to "all the treasures of wisdom and knowledge" that are in God (Col. 2:3)? It is a web of folly. Oh how we should strive to know this God!

When the queen of Sheba heard of Solomon's extraordinary wisdom, she came from the utmost parts of the earth to meet him. Well, someone greater than Solomon is here. God's "understanding is infinite" (Ps. 147:5). "There is no searching of his understanding" (Isa. 40:28). Indeed, it is bottomless, so it can never be searched or sounded. Some people exhaust their brains, consume their bodies, and waste their estates in pursuit of the knowledge of nature. Yet after their striving, they are still at a loss. For all the knowledge they attain, they remain learned fools. What should we be prepared to do for the knowledge of the God of nature—the mighty possessor of heaven and earth? What should we be prepared to sacrifice to know God in comparison to whom all things are less than nothing? What should we be prepared to give for the knowledge of God who will make us wise unto salvation? This is the only knowledge worth seeking, getting, and prizing. "Thus saith the LORD, Let not the wise man glory in his wisdom, neither let the mighty man glory in his might, let not the rich man glory in his riches" (Jer. 9:23). Worldly knowledge, strength, and wealth are not worth glorying in. So what is? "But let him that glorieth glory in this, that he understandeth and knoweth me, that I am the LORD" (Jer. 9:24). This is a rare jewel in which to glory.

There is excellence in all knowledge. It is the eye of the soul to direct its motions. It is the light of the soul to guide its actions. Without knowledge, the soul is a dungeon of darkness and blackness—full of confusion and terror. But there is incomparable excellence in the knowledge of the incomparable God. The object elevates and heightens the act. That is why there is a vast difference between the knowledge of earthly things and heavenly things.

Take note of what kind of knowledge this is. It is not a mere notional or speculative knowledge—although a knowledge of apprehension is necessary (Eph. 5:17). It is an experimental knowledge: "In the hidden part thou shalt make me to know wisdom" (Ps. 51:6). The heart is called the "hidden part" because God alone knows it (1 Kings 8:39). It is such a knowledge that affects the heart with love for Him, fear of Him, and hatred for whatever is contrary to Him. True knowledge takes the heart as well as the head. "He that saith, I know him, and keepeth not his commandments, is a liar, and the truth is not in him" (1 John 2:4). Right knowledge begins in the head, but it does not end there. It affects the heart and regulates the life. Paul prays, "That ye might be filled with the knowledge of his will in all wisdom and spiritual understanding" (Col. 1:9). Why? "That ye might walk worthy of the Lord unto all pleasing, being fruitful in every good work" (v. 10).

CHAPTER 38

Sanctifying Knowledge

The true knowledge of God is a sanctifying knowledge. Holiness is the image of the incomparable God. It was our primitive perfection which we lost at the fall. It is renewed through the knowledge of God. How? Knowledge is the eye by which we see God, and this vision causes assimilation to Him. "But we all, with open face beholding as in a glass the glory of the Lord, are changed into the same image from glory to glory, even as by the Spirit of the Lord" (2 Cor. 3:18). We often change our opinions, attitudes, fashions, and dispositions because of those with whom we associate. Surely then our acquaintance with the holy God will make us in some measure resemble Him.

Other knowledge pollutes the soul. Oftentimes, the more people look into the mysteries of nature, the more they forget the God of nature. They see so much of the operations of nature that they ascribe the principal efficiency to the instrument. For this reason, the wisdom of the wisest in this world is folly (1 Cor. 3:19).

"Professing themselves to be wise, they became fools" (Rom. 1:22). The apostle Paul speaks of the heathen who were estranged from the life of God (a holy life) through their ignorance (Eph. 4:18). But the knowledge of God purifies the soul. As the sun conveys heat with its light, grace is multiplied through the knowledge of God (2 Peter 1:2). After Moses had conversed with God on the mountain, his face shone so much that the Israelites could not look at him (Ex. 34:29–35). When we are acquainted with the blessed God, our lives will shine with holiness. For this reason, David counsels Solomon to know the God of his fathers and serve Him with a "perfect heart" and "willing mind" (1 Chron. 28:9).

The knowledge of God renders sin abominable. The miseries that befall us in our reputations, bodies, and families, plus all the curses of the law and torments of the damned, fall short of revealing the deformed nature of sin. Job abhors himself for his sin (Job 42:6). Why? He explains, "I have heard of thee by the hearing of the ear: but now mine eye seeth thee" (Job 42:5). That is to say, he had some knowledge of God before, but now he had a fuller knowledge of Him. The more we know the greatest good, the more we hate the greatest evil.

The knowledge of God also renders the world contemptible. No one can properly value the creature without a sight of the Creator. No one can trample on the riches, honors, and pleasures of this world without knowing God, who is the riches, honors, and pleasures of the other world. Those who have never seen the sun are amazed at a candle. Likewise, those who have never known the blessed God are fond of pitiful things on earth. But the whole world becomes a dunghill when we behold the incomparable God. Moses refused the pleasures and treasures of Pharaoh's home and preferred the reproaches of Christ because he knew the incomparable God (Heb. 11:25–27).

The knowledge of God also renders God honorable. The more we know sin, the more we loathe it. The more we know ourselves, the more we abhor ourselves. But the more we know God, the more we admire Him. The reason for all our affronts to God is our ignorance of Him. Christ declares, "O righteous Father, the world hath not known thee" (John 17:25). What is the result of this ignorance? "The whole world lieth in wickedness" (1 John 5:19). But when we know God, we find infinite reason to love, fear, honor, and please Him.

Finally, the knowledge of God makes us humble. We are never so low in our own eyes as when we see the incomparable God. The more we know the most holy God (in comparison to whom we are nothing), the more we abase ourselves. David was acquainted with the excellency of God: "O LORD our Lord, how excellent is thy name in all the earth! who hast set thy glory above the heavens" (Ps. 8:1). As a result, he had low thoughts of himself: "What is man, that thou art mindful of him? and the son of man, that thou visitest him?" (v. 4). What a poor, pitiful, contemptible thing is man! What a vain, empty, insignificant nothing is the son of man! The holiest man abhors himself for his lack of holiness in the presence of the most holy God. "Yea, the stars are not pure in his sight. How much less man, that is a worm? and the son of man, which is a worm?" (Job 25:5–6). A worm is the most contemptible creature. All animals trample on it. That is what we are like in our own estimation when we understand the incomparable God.

When Isaiah saw the Lord of Hosts, he cried, "Woe is me! for I am undone" (Isa. 6:5). He never saw so much of his own uncleanness as when he saw God, in whose presence the heavens are unclean. Other knowledge puffs up (1 Cor. 8:1), but the knowledge of God shrinks and shrivels us to nothing.

CHAPTER 39

Satisfying Knowledge

The true knowledge of God is a satisfying knowledge. Our knowledge of creatures cannot satisfy us because it does not correspond to our heaven-born spiritual and immortal soul. The greatest students who have exhausted their brains and bodies in the search of nature's secrets have found by experience that "in much wisdom is much grief: and he that increaseth knowledge increaseth sorrow" (Eccl. 1:18).

The knowledge that satisfies must be suitable in its spirituality to the nature of the soul, in its sufficiency to the various needs of the soul, and in its immortality to the eternal duration of the soul. If the soul lacks any of these, it cannot receive satisfaction. Without these, the soul cannot be perfectly happy. Until it finds what can make it perfectly happy, it will be restless. If it finds an object that is suitable to its nature but not its needs, it will still complain. If it finds an object that is suitable to its nature and needs but is not eternal, it will still be troubled. Because it is incorruptible and immortal, the soul can only desire that good which parallels its own life.

Nothing in this world is suitable to the soul's nature. The soul is spiritual, but the things of this world are physical. The soul's needs are spiritual (pardon of sin, peace of conscience, etc.), but the good things of this life are material. Nothing in this world is suitable to the soul's duration. It will continue forever, but this world will pass away. But God is perfect in all these respects, and He will satisfy our souls. God is a spiritual good and is so suitable to the nature of the soul. He is a universal good, so He can meet the soul's many needs. He is an eternal good, so He is equal to the soul's duration. For these reasons, David tells us that he is fully pleased that God is his portion (Ps. 16:5–6).

If we give a man what he wants and needs, he is content. But if we give him what he wants but does not need, he is discontent. Why? He cannot be content when he has what he wants because his lusts are insatiable. Sinful desires are never satisfied. But if we give someone what he wants and needs (his desires rectified), he is at ease.

When God is the object of our delight, we are at ease. We are not satiated because He is an object too great for our faculties to comprehend, but we are satisfied. When we drink of the "fountain of living waters," we no longer thirst after other objects (Jer. 2:13). Our knowledge of this incomparable God diffuses a sweet peace and calmness into the soul and gives us a ravishing foretaste of what awaits us in the other life.

CHAPTER 40

Saving Knowledge

The true knowledge of God is a saving knowledge. In the other world God knows those who know Him in this world. He owns them: "I will set him on high, because he hath known my name" (Ps. 91:14). God will set us as high as heaven because we know His name on earth. It is worth as much as heaven to know this incomparable God: "And this is life eternal, that they might know thee the only true God, and Jesus Christ, whom thou hast sent" (John 17:3). Knowing the true God and Jesus Christ in this life is the dawn of heaven but not yet the full day; it is the bud of glory but yet not the fruit; and it is the seed of the inheritance but not yet the harvest. This knowledge is of the same nature, though not the same measure, with knowledge in the other world (Eph. 4:13). Now we know as a child, but then we will know as an adult. Now we see God as at a distance through the glass of faith, but then we will see God face to face. "For now we see through a glass, darkly; but then face to face: now I know in part; but then shall I know as also I am known" (1 Cor. 13:12).

CHAPTER 41

The Means of Attaining Knowledge

How do we attain this knowledge of the incomparable God? First, we must acknowledge our ignorance. Conceited students are poor learners. Why? They never look to others for instruction because they think they know everything. "Seest thou a man wise in his own conceit? there is more hope of a fool than of him" (Prov. 26:12). This is what locked the Pharisees in the dark dungeon of ignorance. They were blind, yet they convinced themselves that they could see (Matt. 23:16–17; John 9:40–41). When ignorance and confidence travel together, a person's condition is helpless. He will not make the effort to read, meditate, or listen. Without these things, it is impossible to know God. A conceited person will never labor for what he thinks he already possesses.

True saving knowledge comes from God: "For the LORD giveth wisdom: out of his mouth cometh knowledge and understanding" (Prov. 2:6). As no one can see the sun by candlelight but by its own light, so no one can know God by the light of nature but by light derived from Him. But the proud will not go to God for knowledge. Only those who are willing to learn are fit for His guidance and direction. "The meek will he guide in judgment: and the meek will he teach his way" (Ps. 25:9). We must, therefore, labor to affect our hearts with our ignorance. This is the first necessary step to knowledge. "Let no man deceive himself. If any man among you seemeth to be wise in this world, let him become a fool, that he may be wise" (1 Cor. 3:18). In other words, if we seem to be knowledgeable, we must become ignorant in our own estimation, so that we might truly be knowledgeable.

Second, we must study the Scriptures. As we behold God's glory in His Word, He transforms us into His likeness (2 Cor. 3:18). As the sight of a man's face helps us to know him, even so God's Word is the greatest means for knowing Him. It is the "key of knowledge" (Luke 11:52) which opens the secrets of heaven to the soul. It is a "lamp" and "light" (Ps. 119:105) which reveals hidden things and directs us in our motions and actions. "With the ancient is wisdom; and in length of days is understanding" (Job 12:12). Yet David had more knowledge than the ancients. Why? The law was his "meditation all the day" (Ps. 119:97).

Third, we must pray for knowledge. A twofold light is necessary for physical sight: a light in the eye (a blind man cannot see) and a light in the air (the best eye cannot see in the dark). Likewise, a twofold light is necessary to see God: the light of the Word and the light of the Spirit. The Word cannot do it without the Spirit, and the Spirit will not do it without the Word. All natural and acquired abilities cannot help one poor soul to obtain a saving knowledge of God. It is God who "teacheth man knowledge" (Ps. 94:10). He alone made light in the first creation, and He alone can cause light in the new creation. "For God, who commanded the light to shine out of darkness, hath shined in our hearts, to give the light of the knowledge of the glory of God in the face of Jesus Christ" (2 Cor. 4:6). He who said, "Let there be light" (Gen. 1:3) when darkness covered the face of the earth can command spiritual light—the knowledge of His glory in the face of Christ. Therefore, the apostle Paul prays for this gift: "That the God of our Lord Jesus Christ, the Father of glory, may give unto you the spirit of wisdom and revelation in the knowledge of him" (Eph. 1:17). We must go to Him for assistance to see. "No man knoweth the Son, but the Father; neither knoweth any man the Father, save the Son, and he to whomsoever the Son will reveal him" (Matt. 11:27). Therefore, we must go to the Sun of Righteousness for the light of the knowledge of God.

We must go to Christ like blind Bartimaeus: "Jesus, thou Son of David, have mercy on me...that I might receive my sight" (Mark 10:47, 51). He will pity us, touch our eyes, and enable us to see the things that lead to peace. Remember His promises. "And I will give them an heart to know me, that I am the LORD" (Jer. 24:7).

"For they shall all know me, from the least of them unto the greatest of them" (Jer. 31:34). We can plead these promises with great hope, for He who uttered them "cannot lie" (Titus 1:2).

When God bid Solomon to ask for whatever he wanted, Solomon asked for wisdom (2 Chron. 1:10). His request "pleased the Lord" (1 Kings 3:10).

> And God said unto him, Because thou hast asked this thing, and hast not asked for thyself long life; neither hast asked riches for thyself, nor hast asked the life of thine enemies; but hast asked for thyself understanding to discern judgment; behold, I have done according to thy words…. And I have also given thee that which thou hast not asked, both riches, and honour. (1 Kings 3:11–13)

When we—sensible of our blindness and darkness—lie at the feet of God, begging for spiritual sight, He is pleased.

> Yea, if thou criest after knowledge, and liftest up thy voice for understanding; if thou seekest her as silver, and searchest for her as for hid treasures; then shalt thou understand the fear of the LORD, and find the knowledge of God. For the LORD giveth wisdom: out of his mouth cometh knowledge and understanding. (Prov. 2:3–6)

Digging is hard work, but we do it when searching for gold or silver. We must employ the same diligence in striving after the knowledge of God.

CHAPTER 42

The Motives for Attaining Knowledge

If this God is so incomparable, then we must choose Him for our portion and take Him for our happiness. Is it possible to hear so much of the incomparableness of God yet not desire Him? We cannot meet an eminent person without wishing he were our friend. We cannot encounter an excellent estate without wishing it were our inheritance. Can we hear of the incomparable God without wishing He were our portion? Can we hear so much of His worth without desiring Him? Is it possible for a rational creature to hear of such bottomless treasure and boundless pleasure without wanting to enjoy it? When we understand the gift of God, we will scorn the highest honors, sweetest delights, and greatest riches, and we will trample upon all the crowns and kingdoms of this world. To that end, we must consider the following.

First, we must consider the content of God's offer. In a word, He offers Himself. He is the greatest good that ever was, ever will be, and ever can be. He is more than heaven and earth. He is the King of kings, the Lord of lords, the God of gods, the blessed and glorious Potentate, the first Cause, the original Being, the self-sufficient, the all-sufficient, the absolutely perfect God. He is the high and lofty One who inhabits eternity—to whom a thousand years are but a moment. His duration is incapable of the least accession. He is boundless in His being, omnipotent in His power, unsearchable in His wisdom, inconceivable in His grace, and infinite in all His perfections. He dwells in light that is inaccessible. Angels (the highest of creatures) veil their faces before Him. The whole creation is less than nothing in comparison to Him. He made all things out of nothing. He supports all things and influences all things. He is all things, and He is infinitely more than all things. He is such a necessary good that we are undone without Him. He is so plentiful a good that we can be perfectly happy in Him (Ps. 144:15). We do not need anything else. He is the heaven of heavens (Ps. 16:11). This God is the well of salvation, the Lord of life, the God of all comfort—a hive of sweetness, paradise of pleasure, and heaven of joy. He is the richest grace, dearest love, surest friend, highest honor, greatest beauty, and fullest joy. He alone can enlarge all the faculties and satisfy all the capacities of a heaven-born soul. God is a good which Christ died to purchase for us (Eph. 2:13; 1 Peter 3:18). Surely, if Christ thought Him worth His blood, He is worthy of our acceptance. God is a universal good—not one good, but all good.

He is riches, honors, pleasures, friends, family, health, life, earth, heaven, and infinitely more. He is an eternal good—a good that will stand by us and abide with us when all other good things fail (Ps. 73:25).

Surely, our hearts should melt in astonishment that this God would offer Himself to us. We can call on Him in the day of distress. We can cry to Him in our dying hour, when our soul stands quivering on our lips, ready to take its flight into the unknown regions of the other world; when our friends and relations stand weeping and wailing beside us but unable to comfort us. We can live without God, but we cannot die peacefully without Him. We must stand or fall before Him. He will pass sentence on our eternal absolution or condemnation. He will assign us to an unchangeable state of life or death. Are you willing to have this God for your portion? What do you say? Will you deprive your precious soul of such a treasure? Will you leave it naked to the cruelty of the devil and the curse of the law? Surely this is enough to draw out our most earnest desires for this incomparable God.

Second, we must consider the terms of God's offer. We might think that so boundless a good will cost us a great deal. But all God requires is that we accept Him in His Son. When we take Him for our happiness, we have Him for our happiness. We give more for food and shelter than we need to give for the great, glorious, incomprehensible, and incomparable God. He does not require anything impossible from us. He does not require us to move mountains, calm oceans, or create worlds. He does not require us to satisfy His justice, fulfill His law, or merit His favor. He has done all this for us through His Son. All He desires is that we accept Him as our God in His Son.

Will you not do it? Can you deny your poor soul such a reasonable request? As the servant said to Naaman, "My father, if the prophet had bid thee do some great thing, wouldest thou not have done it? how much rather then, when he saith to thee, Wash, and be clean?" (2 Kings 5:13). I say the same to you. If God were to command you to perform the greatest things imaginable, would you not strive to do them? But all He commands is this: "Thou shalt have no other gods before me" (Ex. 20:3). This commandment contains the sum of your duty and happiness. We must take the true God in Christ for our God, prize Him as our God, love Him as our God, honor Him as our God, and obey Him as our God. When we do, He will be our God forever. We must do for the true God what the covetous man does for his wealth and what the greedy man does for his belly. They give their highest esteem, choicest affection, and greatest service to that which they take for their god. Surely, the true God is more worthy of our devotion.

Third, we must consider the ends of God's offer. I do not want you to think that God is urgent for us to accept Him because He has some need of us. It is purely for our eternal good that He offers Himself to us. He does not need our service any more than He needs the service of the damned and demons. Our righteousness does not help Him, and our wickedness does not hurt Him (Job 22:3; 35:2). He offers Himself to us so that He might be bountiful to us. He seeks our good, not His own. The joy of accepting Him or the misery of rejecting Him is ours (Prov. 9:12). Merchants use arguments to convince their customers to buy their products so that they can enrich themselves. But God calls us to buy from Him— not to enrich Himself (He is as rich as He can be), but so we can enrich ourselves. It is entirely for our good—that we might escape hell and death and attain heaven and life—that God is pleased to offer Himself to us.

What do you think about God's offer? Will you take Him as your portion? Is there anything unreasonable in His terms? Does not your eternal happiness depend on your acceptance of Him? You will have an eternal portion—good or bad. The ungodly man's portion of good things and the godly man's portion of evil things are in this world. But both have immortal souls, and their souls must have immortal portions to abide with them forever. If you prefer the world before God and love the creature above Him and please your flesh more than Him, He will rain on you "fire and brimstone, and an horrible tempest: this shall be the portion of their cup" (Ps. 11:6). But if you accept God in His Son (for there is no making God your friend without Christ) for your chief good and happiness—when all your friends leave you, closest relations forsake you, and your flesh and heart fail you—God will be the strength of your portion forever (Ps. 73:26). Friend, consider what I have said, and may the Lord give you understanding.

CHAPTER 43

Praising God

If God is incomparable, then we must praise Him for His incomparable excellencies. "Praise him according to his excellent greatness" (Ps. 150:2). But what tongue (human or angelic) can do so? It is true we cannot praise God to the utmost of His excellencies, but we can praise Him to the utmost of our abilities. We can give Him our highest praises: "Let the high praises of God be in their mouth" (Ps. 149:6). And we can give Him our greatest praises: "Great is the LORD, and greatly to be praised" (Ps. 145:3). Low praise is an insult to Him, for He is so infinitely great. "According to thy name, O God, so is thy praise unto the ends of the earth" (Ps. 48:10). Since God's name is excellent, His praise must be excellent (Ps. 148:13). David declares, "But I will hope continually, and will yet praise thee more and more" (Ps. 71:14). David had already praised God, but he desires to praise Him more. Similarly, we should ascend in our praise until we come to the highest degree that is possible.

We praise God for His incomparable being. He is perfect, independent, incomprehensible, omnipresent, eternal, and infinite. This should greatly affect our hearts. "Praise ye the LORD. Praise, O ye servants of the LORD, praise the name of the LORD. Blessed be the name of the LORD from this time forth and for evermore. From the rising of the sun unto the going down of the same the LORD's name is to be praised" (Ps. 113:1–3). Why? "The LORD is high above all nations, and his glory above the heavens. Who is like unto the LORD our God, who dwelleth on high" (vv. 4–5).

We praise God for His incomparable attributes. He is incomparable in His power: "O LORD God of hosts, who is a strong LORD like unto thee?" (Ps. 89:8). He is incomparable in His holiness: "Who is like unto thee, O LORD, among the gods? who is like thee, glorious in holiness?" (Ex. 15:11). He is incomparable in His mercy: "Who is a God like unto thee, that pardoneth iniquity, and passeth by the transgression of the remnant of his heritage? he retaineth not his anger forever, because he delighteth in mercy" (Mic. 7:18).

We praise God for His incomparable works. "Oh that men would praise the LORD for his goodness, and for his wonderful works to the children of men!" (Ps. 107:8). Specifically, we praise Him for His works of creation and providence (Job 38:4–7; Ps. 97:8–9). We praise Him especially for His work of redemption:

"Blessed be the Lord God of Israel; for he hath visited and redeemed his people" (Luke 1:68).

We praise God for His incomparable Word. "Thy testimonies are wonderful" (Ps. 119:129). How often does the sweet singer of Israel praise God for His Word? "He sheweth his word unto Jacob, his statutes and his judgments unto Israel. He hath not dealt so with any nation: and as for his judgments, they have not known them. Praise ye the LORD" (Ps. 147:19–20).

What does it mean to praise God?

First, we praise God by admiring Him. We wonder at His being. What manner of God is this? He knows no bounds, no beginning, no succession, and no addition. An amazing admiration of Him is a high commendation of Him. Indeed, our silent wondering at His perfections is almost all the worship we can give Him. When we set ourselves to praise Him, we are struck with amazement at His matchless being and beauty, His infinite excellencies and perfections. Lacking words to express our praise, we sit down in a silent admiration of Him. He is from everlasting to everlasting. He is the cause and original of all things. He is what He is in one indivisible point of eternity.

We wonder at God's attributes. We admire His holiness: "Behold, he put no trust in his servants; and his angels he charged with folly" (Job 4:18). We admire His wisdom: "O the depth of the riches both of the wisdom and knowledge of God!" (Rom. 11:33). We admire

His love: "Behold, what manner of love the Father hath bestowed upon us" (1 John 3:1). We admire His power: "Who is a strong LORD like unto thee?" (Ps. 89:8).

We wonder at God's works. We wonder at the rare works of human artists, but their works are trifles in comparison to the works of the mighty possessor of heaven and earth. "O LORD, how manifold are thy works!" (Ps. 104:24). What a work is creation! It is marvelous and mysterious. The heavens declare His glory, and the earth is full of His goodness (Ps. 19:1; 104:24). What a work is providence! How many rarities, curiosities, and mysteries are wrapped up in it (Ps. 77:19)? What a work is redemption! It is a masterpiece—a work into which the angels desire to look (1 Peter 1:12).

We wonder at God's words. When we hear His Word, we perceive a majesty and authority accompanying it. The very officers who were sent to arrest Christ wondered at His words: "Never man spake like this man" (John 7:46).

Second, we praise God by speaking highly of Him. If God's name alone is excellent, then we must be careful not to take His name in vain. Our apprehensions of Him must be high, and our expressions of Him must be honorable. Our tongue is our glory, because with it we glorify God (Ps. 57:8). We must never speak of God rashly or randomly. Our expressions of Him and to Him must be suitable to His vast perfections. "Ascribe ye greatness unto our God" (Deut. 32:3). We speak honorably of His being: "Who is like unto thee, O LORD, among the gods? who is like thee, glorious in holiness, fearful in praises, doing wonders?" (Ex. 15:11). We speak honorably of His attributes (Ps. 68:34)—His power, mercy, truth, justice, wisdom, and holiness. We speak honorably of His works: "Among the gods there is none like unto thee, O Lord; neither are there any works like unto thy works" (Ps. 86:8). We speak honorably of His Word (Ps. 19:7–10).

Third, we praise God by walking closely with Him. The psalmist declares, "All nations whom thou hast made shall come and worship before thee, O Lord; and shall glorify thy name. For thou art great, and doest wondrous things: thou art God alone" (Ps. 86:9–10). This God must have incomparable obedience: "Be still, and know that I am God" (Ps. 46:10). We must be still, meaning we must cease to offend Him. Why? He is incomparable in knowledge and acquainted with all our ways—private and public. He is incomparable in holiness and hates our wickedness. He is incomparable in power and is able to avenge Himself. He is incomparable in justice and will by no means clear the guilty. He is incomparable in mercy and will receive prodigals who—sensible of their folly and filthiness—return to Him in the Son of His love. We must be still, know that He is God, and obey His laws. Such obedience makes the excellencies of this incomparable God visible to the world (1 Peter 2:9).

CHAPTER 44

The Motives for Praising God

In order to give God the praise of His incomparable perfections, we must consider the following. First, God is incomparably excellent. "Shall not his excellency make you afraid?" (Job 13:11). What honor is due to someone who is excellent? Can our highest honor be high enough and our greatest praise great enough?

Second, God is so incomparably excellent that even angels veil their faces in His presence. The cherubim and seraphim are spotless in their natures and faultless in their lives. As God's special favorites, they are allowed to wait on Him continually and enjoy Him fully and perfectly. Yet they veil their faces before Him. "I saw also the Lord sitting upon a throne, high and lifted up, and his train filled the temple. Above it stood the seraphim: each one had six wings; with twain he covered his face, and with twain he covered his feet, and with twain he did fly" (Isa. 6:1–2). The face of an angel is full of beauty and brightness. It is most excellent. Yet angels are ashamed of their faces before God, who alone is excellent.

Third, God is so incomparably excellent that He humbles Himself to take notice of His perfect angels in heaven. It is not only great condescension on His part to observe the highest and holiest people on earth, but it is boundless humiliation for Him to look upon the principalities and powers in heaven: "Who is like unto the LORD our God, who dwelleth on high, who humbleth himself to behold the things that are in heaven, and in the earth!" (Ps. 113:5–6).

Fourth, God is so incomparably excellent that He is above His creatures' highest adoration. Worship is the most honorable of our works. Praising God is the most honorable act of worship. The angels and elders fall on their faces before the throne: "Blessing, and honour, and glory, and power, be unto him that sitteth upon the throne" (Rev. 5:13). But this incomparably excellent God is above all this worship. He is not above it in the sense of despising it, but exceeding it. "Blessed be thy glorious name, which is exalted above all blessing and praise" (Neh. 9:5).

Fifth, God is so incomparably excellent that His excellencies are beyond the understanding of humans and angels. His excellency is not only beyond our expressions but above our apprehensions. His works are unsearchable (Rom. 11:33). "Lo, he goeth by me, and I see him not; he passeth on also, but I perceive him not" (Job 9:11). If we cannot apprehend God's works, how much less can we understand His nature?

In some respects, His works are finite—terminated on limited beings. Therefore, they are obvious to our senses. But His essence is in all respects infinite. It is beyond our senses. God dwells in unapproachable light (1 Tim. 6:16). As no human eye can behold the sun in its full strength, so no human mind can apprehend the incomparable God in His full beauty and brightness, His boundless excellency and perfection. God says to Moses: "Thou canst not see my face: for there shall no man see me, and live" (Ex. 33:20). No one can behold God in His infinite essence and to the utmost of His perfections without crumbling to nothing.

If God is so incomparably excellent, then what praise, honor, and glory should we give to Him? We are unable to give Him all the glory that is due His name, but we can give Him all that our mind, heart, and affections have to offer. "Bless the LORD, O my soul: and all that is within me, bless his holy name" (Ps. 103:1).

CHAPTER 45

Incomparably Blessed

In conclusion, the doctrine that God is incomparable is useful to God's people by way of comfort. When we take the incomparable God as our God, we are incomparably blessed. People are as happy or miserable as the god whom they serve, for nothing can provide more happiness than it has in itself. Those who serve the flesh as their god are miserable (Rom. 16:18; Phil. 3:18) because their god is vile, weak, deceitful, and transitory (Pss. 49:20; 73:25; Isa. 31:3; Jer. 17:9). Similarly, those who prize the world as their god are miserable because their god is vain, troublesome, uncertain, and fleeting (Eccl. 1:2–3; 5:10; 1 Cor. 7:29–31; 1 Tim. 6:9–10). But those who have an interest in this great God are happy: "Happy is that people, whose God is the LORD" (Ps. 144:15). Why are we incomparably blessed?

First, this incomparable God is ours. We have a title to Him. This is the great privilege of heaven's favorites: "Behold, the tabernacle of God is with men, and he will dwell with them, and they shall be his people, and God himself shall be with them, and be their God" (Rev. 21:3). This is the great promise—the sum and substance of all the promises: "[I] will be their God, and they shall be my people" (Jer. 31:33). This is the great prayer of all who know how to pray (Ex. 33:15; Ps. 4:6; Jer. 14:8). This is the great purchase of the Son of God (1 Peter 3:18). This promise is heaven—the very heaven of heavens. It is not the place but God's presence that makes heaven to be heaven. "In thy presence is fulness of joy; at thy right hand there are pleasures for evermore" (Ps. 16:11). This is the highest and greatest gift which the infinite God can give to us. He can give us greater things than riches, honors, friends, and relations. He can give us greater things than Sabbaths, sacraments, and seasons of grace. He can give us greater things than pardon of sin and peace of conscience. But He cannot give us anything greater than Himself. Oh how sweet are the words when we may call Him "my God"! "Him that overcometh will I make a pillar in the temple of my God, and he shall go no more out: and I will write upon him the name of my God, and the name of the city of my God, which is new Jerusalem, which cometh down out of heaven" (Rev. 3:12).

Oh what a reason to triumph in our happiness—the infinite God is ours! Perhaps we are without honors, friends, family, liberty, peace, health, or strength, but God is ours. He is more than all these things, and He is ours. Our estate is not ours (Hos. 2:9; Hag. 2:8); neither is our family (Ezek. 16:20–21). Our body is not ours (1 Cor. 6:16); neither is our soul (Ezek. 18:3–4). But God is ours—our "exceeding joy" (Ps. 43:4).

Second, the excellencies of this incomparable God are ours. "All [things] are yours" (1 Cor. 3:22). God's incomparable attributes are ours. His incomparable power is ours to protect us (Gen. 15:1; Ex. 15:9–12). His incomparable wisdom is ours to direct us (Ps. 73:23–24). His incomparable mercy is ours to assist us in our miseries (Judg. 10:16). His incomparable grace is ours to pardon all our iniquities (Ex. 34:6–7; Mic. 7:18). His incomparable love is ours to refresh and delight our soul (Ps. 21:5–6). His incomparable justice is ours to accept us as righteous for the sake of His Son (Rom. 3:24). His incomparable faithfulness is ours to fulfill all the gracious promises that He has made to us (Ps. 89:33–34). His incomparable majesty is ours to render us glorious forever (Isa. 43:4; Ezek. 16:14). His incomparable joys and pleasures are ours to satisfy us (Ps. 36:8; Matt. 25:21). His incomparable works are ours—His works of creation (Ps. 37:11), providence (Rom. 8:28), and redemption (John 10:15; Gal. 2:20; Rev. 1:5–6). His incomparable Word is ours, making us wise to salvation: "For whatsoever things were written aforetime were written for our learning, that we through patience and comfort of the scriptures might have hope" (Rom. 15:4).

Third, the excellencies of this incomparable God are ours forever. God's incomparable eternity is ours, and so long as He is God He will be our God. When the unbeliever's god is gone, our God remains. When all our honors, riches, friends, and relations leave us, our God will abide with us: "For this God is our God forever and ever" (Ps. 48:14). He is not our God for a day, week, month, year, or age, but "forever and ever." He is not our God for a thousand years, but "forever and ever." He is not our God for as many ages as there are stars in heaven, drops in the sea, and creatures on the earth, but "forever and ever." This God is our God forever and ever! Our immortal soul has an immortal God—an immortal good. We will be forever with this incomparable God. This comforts us in the midst of all the persecutions and afflictions that befall us in this world.

> For the Lord himself shall descend from heaven with a shout, with the voice of the archangel, and with the trump of God: and the dead in Christ shall rise first: then we which are alive and remain shall be caught up together with them in the clouds, to meet the Lord in the air: and so shall we ever be with the Lord. Wherefore comfort one another with these words. (1 Thess. 4:16–18)

Some other
Puritan Resources

from
**REFORMATION
HERITAGE BOOKS**

The Fading of the Flesh and the Flourishing of Faith

George Swinnock
Edited by J. Stephen Yuille

978-1-60178-072-0 Paperback, 184 pages

The Puritans frequently talked about dying well. That is something we do not discuss much these days, though we should. Expounding Psalm 73:26, "My flesh and my heart faileth: but God is the strength of my heart, and my portion for ever," Swinnock combines careful explanation with vivid illustration to reveal the futility of earthly comforts and to highlight the inestimable comfort, satisfaction, and joy afforded us in Christ.

"This wonderful little book, written with charm, simplicity, and clarity by George Swinnock is bound to prove both a delight and a challenge to any Christian who values the riches of the gospel. It is a spiritual gem that deserves to be read and re-read. In addition, its charm, simplicity, and clarity make it a perfect entry point to the writings of the pastoral Puritans. Beautifully edited for the modern reader by Dr. Stephen Yuille, *The Fading of the Flesh* is a rare spiritual treat."

—Sinclair B. Ferguson, professor of systematic theology, Redeemer Theological Seminary

"Trading and Thriving in Godliness":
The Piety of George Swinnock

Edited and Introduced by J. Stephen Yuille

978-1-60178-041-6   Paperback, 235 pages

In *"Trading and Thriving in Godliness,"* J. Stephen Yuille highlights George Swinnock's conviction that godliness is the primary employment of every Christian. Yuille begins the book by analyzing the influences on, groundwork for, and expressions of piety in Swinnock's life and thought. The remainder of the book presents fifty selections from Swinnock's writings that exemplify his teaching on the foundation, value, pursuit, nature, and means of godliness, as well as its motives.

"Swinnock gives us the essence of Puritanism, and J. Stephen Yuille gives us the essence of Swinnock. Here are doctrine and life, vision and devotion, the poetry and the passion of typical Puritan preaching. A first-rate taster of what is available in Swinnock's *Works*."

—Peter Lewis, author of *The Genius of Puritanism*

Suffering and Sovereignty:
John Flavel and the Puritans on Afflictive Providence

Brian H. Cosby
Foreword by Gerald Bray

978-1-60178-197-0   Paperback, 176 pages

Brian H. Cosby examines Flavel's teachings on suffering and how that theology translated into practical application for suffering believers. Serious consideration is given to issues related to the origin and nature of suffering, how it relates to divine sovereignty, God's purpose for it, how people were encouraged to respond to it, and the benefits of comfort and consolation such understandings produce in believers. Cosby ably gathers these elements together so as to present a Puritan theology of suffering drawn from Flavel's writings.

"This book, filled with provocative quotes from Flavel and ably arranged and explicated by Cosby, helps us understand Flavel's pastoral advice for how Christians might view these seasons of suffering."

—Kelly M. Kapic, coeditor of *The Devoted Life: An Invitation to Puritan Classics*